My spiritual Journey in Search of universal Truth

Maria Toonen

Serebrov Boeken
The Hague

ISBN: 9789083267623; 978-90-832676-2-3
Translator: Ms. Joy Kearney
Editor: Gouri Gozalov c.s.
Ilustrations: Tatiana Spasolomskaya
Design: Maria Toonen en Gouri Gozalov

© Serebrov Boeken, Den Haag, 2022
Publisher: Guram Kochi
Tel.: +31 (0) 70 352 15 65
E-mail: serebrovboeken@planet.nl
Website: www.serebrovboeken.nl

All rights reserved. No part of this publication may be reproduced or transmitted in any form or by any means, electronic or mechanical, including photocopy and recording, or stored in a retrieval system, without the written permission of the publisher.

TABLE OF CONTENTS

Foreword from the publisher 4
Foreword from the author 5
Introduction 6
Chapter 1. 1937 – 1950. The beginning. Former Dutch
Colonial Indonesia. War. Journey to Holland.. 8
Chapter 2. 1950-1965. Becoming an adult in Holland.
Living in Italy. The first mystic experiences 24
Chapter 3. 1965 – 1975. In Holland. Theosophy. Astrology 35
Chapter 4. 1975 – 1983. The Findhorn Community
in Scotland. Anthroposophy. Gurdjieff 43
Chapter 5. 1983 – 1989. Tour through the sacred places
of India. First contact with the Sufism of Hazrat Inayat Khan.
Aura- and chakra healing. The dancing dervishes in Konya,
Turkey 46
Chapter 6. 1989: Meeting with three spiritual Russians 76
Chapter 7. The three Russians: more concerning
their teachings and their spiritual background 115
Chapter 8. The Freemasons 125
Chapter 9. Contemplations 133
Chapter 10. Faust in the twenty first century.
The new Hermeticism: the magician seeking God 140
Chapter 11. Russian Orthodoxy - Thoughts 147
Chapter 12. Conclusion. Monday, 5 March 2007 162

FOREWORD FROM THE PUBLISHER

This book is an autobiography, in which the author relates her experiences during her lifelong search for a higher meaning of life. This is the voice of an extraordinary soul, who felt at home in Indonesia, the Netherlands, Italy, Russia, Tibet, India, ancient Egypt and at the same time nowhere. The doors to higher positions in a number of esoteric spiritual hierarchies appeared to be open to her. She was able to penetrate through to the mystic core of these spiritual messages, but she aspired only to modest positions, somewhere in the background and after a while she departed again to follow her own Path. In the middle of the lively atmosphere of the established, esoteric schools she continued to ask herself where her soul's real home was. Her love of Christ, planted in her by her father just before he died in the war, appeared to be an invisible thread and all her knowledge and insights, collected from the various spiritual traditions, were united in this way.

Guram Kochi
The Hague, May 2009

FOREWORD FROM THE AUTHOR

My friends say that I, as seeker of truth, should write down my accounts of my religious quests and my experiences in various esoteric schools. And furthermore, that I should recount about my travels, my pilgrimages. I should write about the confrontations and conflicts, that I experienced both internally and externally, and try to find the essence of my spiritual development, my quest for God.
Many people are seeking inner light, God, and thinking about the mystery of life: who are we and where are we going? Many become aware of a greater, creative and inspiring inner and outer life and this is what I want to tell you about.

This book is an autobiography and most of the names have been changed.

Maria Toonen
The Hague, 28th May 2010

INTRODUCTION

With what purpose have I yet again been incarnated in this life? Why have I allowed myself to be conceived on the Indian Ocean, when my parents were on tropical leave and on a boat from the former Dutch Indonesian colony to Holland?

Now, at a respectable age, I look back on my life and ask myself seriously: 'have I achieved the objective I intended?' I remember that as a young girl of eleven I once said to someone: 'I want to know a great deal in my life and be able to help others'. Was that a memory of a distant past? Of former lives? Have I succeeded in doing this, with just a few lectures, Builder's pieces, articles I have written, contacts I have had, my ideals? I became familiar with and was a member/student of a number of esoteric schools, at which I gratefully absorbed the knowledge and meanwhile, in order to do something in return, made myself useful. Later I departed, disappointed and sometimes conflicted, because I apparently was not yet ripe enough to be able to come to terms wisely with certain situations. I received a great deal of knowledge and shared this with others, but asked myself if this really improved the quality of my life and theirs? Did I miss something? My ideal and the knowledge and the ecstasy were very far removed from the reality of my life. Or was the theosopher from California indeed right, when she told me in 2002, in South Africa, that the three years that I had spent in the Japanese concentration camp, as with many others like myself, had caused psychological damage, and that it expresses itself in the form that one frequently is not in a position to press on just a little longer or finish what was started. According to her there then followed a breaking point and the situation would be terminated sooner or later. She may be right, but I did not take her remark very seriously, because in my life I have had many changing situations and circumstances (working environments, marriages, memberships of various organisations etc.). This concerned longer periods of time as well, and I did not see these as lost pieces of the puzzle of time. Quite the opposite, in fact, I am even happy about this variation, because the reality of life for me is that it is constantly 'transient', growing, streaming, and never static like 'still water' for example. But let us investigate this.

* * *

Chapter 1. 1937 – 1950. The beginning. Former Dutch Colonial Indonesia. War. Journey to Holland

I was born a couple of years before the Second World War in the former Dutch 'Indies' (now Indonesia), in Semarang in Central Java, with, according to my horoscope: the sun in Pisces, the moon in Virgo and Leo ascending. Since my parents, Adelbert Toonen and Dorothee van Hof were Dutch, I am what is known as a 'totok', the nickname for someone born in Indonesia of Dutch parents.

After the Japanese invaded in 1942 I was placed in a Japanese concentration camp, Lampersari, near Semarang, together with my mother, my younger sister, Marjolein , along with several hundred women and children. My father was a prisoner of war, after the invasion of the Japanese in 1942 he was captured after four days of battle by the Dutch and the Indonesian armies against the dominance of the Japanese army and ended up in a concentration camp. He died just before the end of the war, on 23 December 1944, in a Japanese camp for men. It must have been close to Batavia (present-day Jakarta) and he is buried there. The War Graves Foundation could not trace his grave a couple of years ago, as it had apparently been destroyed, and I have therefore had my father's name included in a memorial book of all fallen Dutchmen in Indonesia.

My sister and I do not remember much about him and we grew up in Holland without a father. As is the case with many children who have lost a father or mother, this was a major blow in terms of our development and transition from child to adult. My father must have had a premonition of it, before the outbreak of war. I once received a page of my father's notebook from my mother, written by my father, and to this day I get tears in my eyes when I read this verse, sadly very pertinent to my family's situation, written by A. Roland Holst (from: 'The plougher'):

I will never more see the proud stems
Nor ever more bind the full sheaves
But let me believe in the harvest
For which I serve

My father and mother went to the Dutch Indies around 1930 with the intention of building a future there. They went to live in Java, in Semarang. They both worked, my father as bookkeeper at a wholesale company and my mother as assistant accountant at another company. They were both very musical and my father, who was still having piano lessons from the famous conductor Eduard van Beinum, regularly gave piano recitals, as a talented amateur, for the Indonesian radio. My mother played violin beautifully and at the beginning of the concentration camp period, when the Japanese still permitted this, she gave concerts on many occasions for the hundreds of women at the Lampersari camp, near Semarang, being accompanied on the piano by her American friend, 'aunt' Rhoda Jongsma, as we called her.

What little I remember of my father is his love for his two daughters, his beautiful piano-playing and his stories about the Bible and about Jesus Christ. He used to read to my sister and I from a children's Bible and play the piano for us. This was always a major event. I remember that we were always very moved when he played and told us a story about a young bird that had flown the nest and afterwards got lost and could not find its way back again. We sobbed on hearing this. My father also frequently played music together with my mother and this has always remained with us as a vague, bright memory. My sister Marion was born at the end of 1938. This took place in the Saint Elizabeth Hospital in Semarang, a Roman Catholic hospital, where the nurses were nuns. It was normal that the nuns took the baby as soon as it was born to have it baptised by the priest, sometimes without the prior explicit permission of the parents. My father, who was brought up as a Catholic and my mother, who was Protestant, were satisfied with this.

My mother told us later that my father, while in the Indies, which is what we called present day Indonesia, had been involved in freemasonry and had become a mason. He was very enthusiastic about it and took it very seriously. She could not share this with him, as women were not permitted to enter the lodge, she told me, and it was not permitted to speak about freemasonry outside the lodge. I was fully aware that my father had been a Freemason when later on in life, in 1995, I too became a member of the Freemasons.

Our small family lived before the outbreak of war in Semarang, in a house with a large garden, which was well-tended by the 'kebon' (the gardener). The lawn always had to be mown to deter snakes and for this purpose we also kept geese. There was baboe Sis and also another baboe to take care of my sister and I and there was a nanny, the djongos (houseboys) and the kokkie or cook. The love that we received from these precious darlings a few years before the outbreak of the war, gave us a warm inner foundation of immeasurable value for our later lives. I am so grateful for this gift from my native land, present-day Indonesia, when my life had just begun. For in the years to follow, from the outbreak of the war, my sister and I were starved of love and safety. This was the case with many others, who found themselves repatriated to Holland after the war, without fathers and mothers, brothers and sisters.

My father had planted his love for Jesus Christ deep in my childhood heart and the awareness of that love, as well as his love for us, has remained with me throughout my life, whether consciously or unconsciously. My parents were not the church-going kind. I think I was the kind of child who was a dreamer and my father was very important to me. His death was therefore a catastrophe, as I quite soon realised. I remember that when my mother told us, at the end of 1944, in the Japanese concentration camp, that my father was dead, my first thought, as a little girl of eight, was: 'Papa, I am not allowed to have a daddy, it's not for me', and I felt something close down inside, as if a door was shut and locked. I shrugged my shoulders a little, hid this truth away somewhere deep inside and consoled my mother with the words: 'Mama, don't cry, isn't Papa in heaven now?' My mother nodded vaguely. My sister sobbed but I had no tears, I couldn't cry. I could never cry throughout my whole life, though I had terrible inner pain and suffering, especially when I had failing or broken relationships and disappointments, inner loneliness, but crying was never an option. This is where the 'Cinderella feeling' came from, that I carried with me throughout my life, as did many others of my generation from the concentration camps, the camp children. You have little or no feeling of self-worth; you have the feeling that 'no-one is backing you' to support you, however your life develops, because your father is not there, you are not worthy of something beautiful, something special, and you don't hold it tightly, you have the tendency to be awkward about it. You do not fight for it. A real 'Cinderella' feeling.

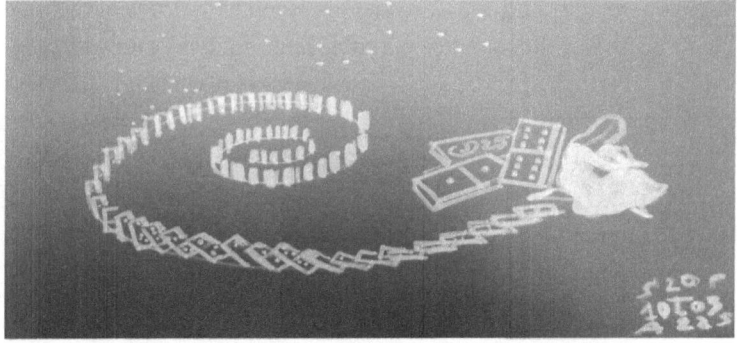

Apart from the camp experiences, our generation of totoks are 'the last of the Mohicans', because after we are all dead there is no-one who can tell stories any more about the good old days, 'tempo doeloe', about our home in our beautiful and much-loved native land of that time, our 'Indies'.

In 1942 we were interred in the Japanese internment camp Lampersari and we remained there for at least three years, until the end of 1945. Before that, after the Japanese invasion of the Indies and the departure of my father, my mother was alone with my sister and I in a house on Srondol, a hill above Semarang. Most Europeans had already left, how and why she was there alone is not clear to me, I was too young, and she had to endure the nightmare of many days of 'rampokkende' (roving and murdering) inlanders, below us, in their kampongs (villages). These poor people went completely mad after the landing of the Japanese and ran amok. They murdered, robbed, plundered, set fires and screamed unceasingly. I remember that still. Later my mother told of how she, as a mother alone, had listened in terror to the screaming, had seen houses burning and knew: 'if they come up here we are finished'. Then she was suddenly and thankfully collected by someone from the government, and we made our way on foot, with our belongings on a cart, to the Japanese camp Lampersari, a concentration camp for women and children. Many people stood by the side of the road and my mother thought it remarkable later on that I suddenly pointed to a distinctive woman in a purple dress and long jet black hair with a fringe who stood there talking and I said: 'look mama, what a strange lady'. The coincidental thing is that this American lady, aunty Rhoda, would become her best friend and would be an immense source of support to her, without whose help and support she would not have survived her time in the camp.

We came to a long street, Sompok, with ditches on both sides of the road, and small stone Indonesian houses. We were lucky that we got a room for the three of us in such a stone house, on Sompok 90, because the houses in the other neighbourhoods (Blimbing, Lombok and Manga) were of wood, just like the little kampong houses of the poor. We lived in our little house, intended for a family of father, mother and child, until the end of the war with forty women and children in total. Women and children were even living on the 'emper', an open corridor with a view onto the courtyard. Every morning there was the morning call and we had to stand in front of our house at seven o'clock, then a couple of Japanese would come along and we had to bow to them. Once I saw in the distance that a sick, malnourished woman, who had been put sitting in a chair by her nurse in front of her house, could not get up to bow. A Jap walked up to her and screamed that she had to bow, but she was too weak to stand up. Then the Jap hit her. The big, strong woman who nursed her and stood beside her became angry and hit the Jap in return. But she should have known better. She was taken away and tortured for three days by the Kempetai, the Japanese SS. Every morning they beat her until she was unconscious, a Japanese doctor would check if she was still alive, if so she was taken outside and laid between large wooden pillars, the pillars were laid over her and then they left her all day in the burning, tropical sun. Every evening she was given something to eat, was permitted to sleep and every morning the abuse began again until the doctor indicated it must stop, because she was almost dead, and then she was brought outside again. This lasted three days, she survived it, but she was just a shadow of what she had previously been.

After I turned eighteen, in Holland, I often had nightmares that I was back in the Jap camp and the planes were flying straight at me and dropping bombs on us. In fact there were planes that flew over our camp that had bombed targets behind and outside of our camp, but I was not the target anymore.
Once, when I was around twenty-eight, I had the same dream and then a bomb did indeed fall on our house and on me and we were crushed. But now for the strange part: I felt obliterated by the bombing, but I noticed that I was still alive, in my consciousness or suchlike. I looked around me in this state and looked at the rubble

I found myself in, and I thought 'is this death then, is this all?' I was not dead as far as I was concerned, though physically I was! That dream and that experience stayed with me for the rest of my life, it made me happy, especially the fact that I was still there, without panic or anxiety. That was a learning experience and gave me, as I later learnt, some knowledge about the hereafter.

My mother had found work in the camp quite quickly at the 'food distribution service'. Every day food was prepared for the approximately seven thousand women and children (I did not know exactly how many there were, my mother was not very clear about this) in enormous cauldrons, and that had to be distributed in an orderly way. The women came with their rentangs (a receptacle with metal dishes that slid on top of each other) to the kitchen to collect the food. The word 'food' was no longer applicable after some time as the tapioca porridge, with the small, slippery transparent balls normally used to make glue, had little resemblance to actual food. I could not swallow those little glue balls. I refused to eat and my mother desperately tried to at least get some food into me. My sister could manage to eat it a bit more easily and I admired her for this... My mother gave us the best lessons she could in reading, writing and calculation, I remember that well.

Towards the end of the war, I was around seven years old, I pressed my finger into my leg and saw that the impression remained in the flesh. I called my mother cheerily and said: 'look, Mama, how funny, when I press my finger on my leg the impressions stay there'. My mother was not happy at all because she knew that this was the beginning of beriberi, malnutrition. The water retention began in the legs and crept upwards and when it reached your heart you died. I knew that as well then. The malnutrition eventually reached my stomach and then the war was over and we had better food, or at least I think that was how it went. I remember the day that planes suddenly flew over our camp, with the Dutch flag painted on the underside. Suddenly the women fetched their strictly forbidden radios from every nook and cranny and listened to the news. During the whole camp time there was severe punishment administered for the possession of a radio.

But when the war was over, it was not entirely over for us. The camps, that were first opened to release people, were then closed for safety reasons, because the womens' camps were regularly attacked by so-called 'heiho' boys. Encouraged and trained by the Japs, these delinquent Indonesian boys of around 18 wanted to fight for their freedom against America and Holland. They attacked the women's camp in their hoards, shouting 'death to America' and singing and shooting, with the objective of murdering all women and children. Something similar happened in a camp near ours. The head of our camp, Mrs van der Poel, arranged that a small number, I think less than ten Jap prisoners of war received the assignment to defend our camp against these hoards of hundreds who were fired up by the Japs. These few Japs were promised that if they succeeded in stopping the attack of the hoards and saving us they would be freed after the war and cease to be prisoners of war. For three days they fought heavily and the handful of Japs fought like lions. It had been said that Japanese soldiers could fight well... My mother was there when, at a given moment, the Japanese commander came to Mrs van der Poel and said that was it, there was no more ammunition. The way my mother told it, they sat for a while in desperation, thinking we were all finished. And then suddenly they heard strange sounds in the distance, like drums. It proved be an English garrison, which was sent by the English and Americans to save us. It was a complete miracle. Afterwards, since we saw the prowess of these ten Japanese, who, as my mother told us, `almost fought to the death', we have never had any more negative feelings after the war towards Japanese. But this does not apply to other women and men from the Japanese camp.

I remember a wild ride in a truck from our camp to the port of Semarang, in 1945. We were to be taken by an American troop transport ship to Batavia (Jakarta) and sheltered there at a barracks until we could leave for Holland. Together with a number of women and children from our camp we were brought in an army vehicle to the troop transport ship. These trucks were also attacked regularly by 'rampokkers' (rovers and arsonists) and heiho boys, especially as it was known there were European women and children in them. A short time before us in East Java an English convoy of a few hundred women and children had been murdered. We also had our challenges, we were promptly attacked. A gunfight broke out and the trucks swerved dangerously to avoid the bullets, driving as fast as possible. I remember that I heard whistling sounds around me, probably the bullets, and that I thought, at the age of eight: 'everyone is acting crazy'. We had to lie on the bottom of the loading bay in order to avoid being hit. Luckily our group all survived the ordeal and we were dropped off at the American troop transport ship. We arrived at the lifeboat deck where my mother tied us to the mast with long ropes because there were no railings and it was therefore dangerous for children. There were also no railings on the rest of the ship and on the voyage there was major drama when two children fell overboard. I still remember the screaming and crying mothers, the searchlights on the water from the coast and the panic regarding the many sharks. I suspect this is why since that time I have never felt very relaxed on the water. My first husband Andries and I had a sailing boat, but I never really enjoyed sailing. That was even more enjoyable for him, because he was a passionate sailor and during his student days he was a sailing instructor at the Loosdrechtse Plassen; he always enjoyed when I became a bit panic stricken at a wave and swayed back and forth. I liked sailing, if the wind was minimal...

We stayed for nine months from 1945-1946 in a barracks in Batavia, called the ninth Battalion, used by soldiers during the war. Even there we were sometimes shot at from outside if we were in the garden, or walking on the emper (open corridor). The extremists were in a large waringin tree just outside the gedèk (surrounding fence) and whenever the shooting began we ran as fast as possible to our beds and crept under them.

In March 1946 we got a place on the overcrowded merchant ship De Bloemfontein that was full of repatriates. I remember our journey through the Suez canal very well, the desert around us was very unusual. Four weeks later we arrived in the port of Amsterdam. I remember our berths, bunks above each other in the enormous space below deck in the ship. I ran up the stairs to listen to the Wilhelmus, played for us on the quayside, and then I ran downstairs again to warm up because it was unbearably cold outside. Our Attaca jackets, that we got during a stop in Attaca, on the Suez canal, were not very warm.

We lost everything during the war, our money, our clothing and other possessions, and came to Holland with only our Attaca clothing and our passports. We stayed a few months in The Hague with a sister of my father, until we found a house in the 'Statenkwartier'. This neighbourhood was a buffer zone during the war, therefore evacuated, and we were the first to rent a house and settle there with a few family members from Leiden. My sister and I went to primary school in the area, on the van Hoornbeekstraat.

The first thing my mother bought was a piano and my sister and I immediately received piano lessons. This was the greatest wish of my father, my mother told us, that Marjolein and I would learn to play the piano. We always took this very seriously and developed into accomplished (amateur) pianists. My sister and I both have grand pianos and play regularly, also together with others. Together with my mother, who played violin beautifully, we played music for many years and gave house concerts, using also recorder or concert flute.

Via her old contacts at KLM my mother got a job there quite quickly and developed into a valued international financial expert. At home the war was rarely mentioned, and my father never was. I regretted that very much later, when I discovered that there was an afterlife and that the dead must not be forgotten. My mother had apparently put the past behind her and did not want to or was unable to talk about it. She always impressed upon us that no matter how much you have had to suffer, 'the spirit triumphs'. She received a lot of strength from this and it has also become my motto in life. We were not religious but we were believers so this motto suited us well.

My sister and I did the entrance exam a few years later for the secondary school, the girls' HBS on the Stadhouderslaan in The Hague. The director of this school was Mrs Prins, who would unexpectedly play an important role in my spiritual life decades later. Her husband was the younger brother of Sufi Hazrat Inayat Khan, and in 1985 I got in touch with the Sufi Circle in The Hague. But I will tell you more about this later.

Regarding the Japanese camp, when I must have been six or eight years old, I still have strange images of a meeting with a very pleasant, stately man with a turban who talked with me and reassured me. I wondered for some time if this had really happened. Was it a dream? Or a half dream, between waking and sleeping? At the end of the war Gurkhas came, English soldiers, to monitor our camp against the attacks of the heiho. When I saw those turbanned men, I went promptly for days in search of that person from my memory and examined closely all the Gurkhas I could find. By their turbans, I could distinguish them easily from the other soldiers. Unfortunately I have never found that one nice man with the turban again. The Gurkhas looked much more rough and did not resemble the beautiful presence of the man with whom I had been chatting. Later this picture returned to me, when in 1964 I was in Italy and busy with Theosophy, and heard of stories concerning the Mahatma of the Himalayas, and concerning the masters Morya and Koot Hoomi.

Our life in Holland began to find its own pace and after the elementary school we went to a girls' secondary school in The Hague. My mother, who had built a career at KLM, was at work all day, and seemed to feel safe that we were at a girls' school. In this way she hoped there would be no 'problems' with boys. The disadvantage was that our mother was always absent and therefore was not there waiting for us with tea when we came from school. It was housekeepers and cleaning ladies, and I remember a Polish housekeeper, who was teased considerably by us, running behind us with buckets of water, which she threw after us as we slipped out the door. We did not get wet, but the wallpaper was soaking.

After our final examination and when we started our adult life, we had therefore hardly any experience with men, outside of the respectable dancing lessons at Ruby Dorani in The Hague. I knew nothing of men and for a long time I had major difficulties with this. You could say, that the picture of our father was overshadowed while we were growing up, this being important for a little girl, only having an image of violent Japs. My image of men had always been of someone hostile and until late in my life I was a little frightened of men with strong personalities, however nice they were. Their energy posed a kind of physical threat and that remained a kind of menace for me. Except if they fulfilled my need for fatherly love and protection. But I have not become any happier as a result, it stayed with me and has, however, produced useful lessons... Gradually I started to get the message.

During my puberty, both at dancing lessons and at the tennis club, I felt attracted to boys who were gentle and friendly. I was good-looking and, due to the nature of my work later as bookkeeper/administrator, found myself surrounded by men. As time went by I found it difficult to hold my own in such an environment, because I usually did not see through the typical men's games played at professional level in the business world. I always did my work with a great deal of pleasure and effort and no-one could do anything about that. But if someone was intrigued by this, either because they were jealous or because I was a woman, I was usually the loser. My low self esteem, the Cinderella from the Jap camp, of which I was not aware for a very long time, was an advantage to my opponents.

Probably due to the psychological damage that we had incurred as a result of the Japanese camp time, I had little difficulty in ending relationships or friendships. In spite of my social activities, my job, and my work in clubs and governing boards, I thrived on loneliness. I had then the feeling that I was `at rest at last' and living from my own perspective. This own perspective was composed up to my fourteenth year of fantasies concerning little people, gnomes and elves that I followed, outside in nature, in their way of life. I also found it possible, generally by day, to lie on my bed and sink into a thoughtful state, without being asleep. Then I experienced all kinds of psychic experiences, something akin to the tales and pictures from old, strange times, which seemed to come to me from the cosmos. My mind was then like an empty projection screen ready to project all kinds of inspiring knowledge and images, perhaps a perception of far flung times... That mood was there.

That loneliness, or perhaps 'solitude', frequently caused me to withdraw into myself and 'create an inner prison', in which I locked myself for a while to protect myself from the outside world. How this works I only later understood, because this compulsion has remained and I must be cautious not to isolate myself too much, because that can cause problems. I am, in fact, very fond of sociability and lively company, and you cannot find this in isolation. I had, especially in my teenage years, many fears, which had intensified in my seventeenth and eighteenth year. I taught myself to come to terms with these panic attacks, however, and discovered that you can act as if the fear is a 'thing', with which you can negotiate and with which you can make agreements, such as: tonight I want to sleep, come back tomorrow, but the inner self continued searching for a possible escape from the disappointing daily awkwardness and misunderstandings. Now I would formulate it in this way: earthly life is in itself always a repetitive process for everyone, as if you are on a treadmill, to which you are bound, in this three-dimensional world. It is like a prison, where you are joined to everyone and everything by some sticky tendrils. If you do your best to throw off these tendrils you have freed yourself and the wide, clear blue sky becomes fully visible. An immense relief! The greatest luck that you can have is to meet someone, who tries to live from that full airy sky, and who wants to communicate with you. You then realise that tremendous freedom, which is within us, and is locked in, and of which we are unfortunately hardly aware. For humanity the great illusion of earthly living, which we do not realise, is that life is the same repetitive spinning top, with always the same plus and minus experiences. In fact I already sought God during my puberty, half consciously, I knew that He would deliver me. Now, with hindsight, I realise with satisfaction that the difficulties of life never forced me `under', and that I always bounced back, just like weeds grow, full of enthusiasm and expectation, to face the adventures of life.

From the age of sixteen onwards I became more and more interested in spiritual subjects and I discovered the books of Paul Brunton, which opened spiritual doors for me. The first book of his that I read was `Secret Egypte', a country that for quite some time held a major attraction for me. Then when I was around fourteen, I read an unforgettable girls' storybook called: `In the shadow of the pyramids'. I really enjoyed this book. I can still feel the excitement that I felt when I was reading it as if I could remember something valuable that I knew of ancient Egypt. I felt something of the mysteries, the wonderful people, sun-drenched buildings and splendid events, in short: I wanted to go there. That did not happen till 1990, but then I was in a completely different Egypt, that of then. From Paul Brunton's book `The yogi of India', I used the breathing and relaxation techniques, which were practised by the yogis, and tried relieving the suffering of a friend, who suffered from fatal bone cancer.

* * *

Chapter 2. 1950-1965. Becoming an adult in Holland. Living in Italy. The first mystic experiences

Returning to that time I remember the years of the primary school, secondary school, training and courses and in 1956, at the tennis club H.S.T.C. (The Hague students tennis club) I met the Delft student, Andries. He was studying physics, with as specialisation nuclear engineering. A turbulent two years followed, full of nice moments as well as conflicts, with an engagement which I broke off a couple of times, but due to the intervention of my mother and manipulation of Andries himself, was always back `on' again. Nevertheless, on 18 August 1958 we married. The night of the wedding I found it impossible to sleep and then just when I succeeded I dreamed that someone said to me `don't worry, it won't last longer than six years'. Well, that appeared to be exactly accurate, as later transpired. After he had completed his studies, a year later, I left my job as a secretary/assistant in material management at an American engineering firm, and in 1960 we left for Italy. He had entered service as a physicist at Euratom in Ispra, at Lake Maggiore.

On 14 May 1961 our son Edwin was born in The Hague, in my mother's house, because we had no fixed place of residence still. The days after the labour I was in ecstasy. I felt that the Mother Goddess of the earth was with me and I realised that I had reached the pinnacle of my life as a woman: I had borne a child and she had supported me. The ecstasy lasted some days. Edwin was joyfully received by his father and I and I knew that everything in my life would revolve around him. The midwife taught me how to look after him. It was a great relief when he could finally speak because then I knew everything was well with him.

We lived in a village, Caldana, in a large old-fashioned, typical Italian villa with one driveway bordered by hydrangea shrubs, about thirteen kilometres from Ispra. I took care of my son, played piano seriously because we had bought a Rösler baby grand in Ispra, to my great joy. I did some oil painting, read a lot from our varied book collection and enjoyed the splendours of nature. We had no television, because it had just come on the market, at least in our part of Italy. Friends had, however, and sometimes we could watch a programme there, such as when my teacher Mozzati gave a concert. But I always thought: 'who would want to watch such an uninteresting box'. I now realise that three years in Italy, with nature, art, living a life full of love, in the years afterwards has proven to be a kind of matrix for my inner life. There was much music in our house, gramophone records of concerts, the splendid mass by Schubert, the music of Bach, his concerts for two piano and orchestra, my own piano playing and still much more...

Nowadays I do not listen to so much classical music any more, and I am ashamed to say my attitude is one of: 'I know all of that already'. I play piano quite a lot, however, because in 1985, I had bought a splendid grand piano in the Netherlands with my savings, a Feurich, which I play as a rather good amateur.

Then, in Caldana, I found an interesting book of my father in our bookcase that had been carefully kept by my mother, despite the war, and she had brought it from Indonesia together with a thick book about J.S. Bach, it was called 'the Great Initiated' by Eduard Schuré. The lives of the founders of the different religions are described and also the life of Jesus. This book captivated me spontaneously and I was unexpectedly moved towards mystic levels with magnificent views and cosmic panoramas. The tales concerning Jesus affected me very deeply. I had my first mystic experiences and I also had at a given moment an experience, which I later saw described, during my Theosophy studies, as 'samadhi'. I experienced some moments in a majestic environment of light, perfect harmony and balance, all antagonism and opposition disappeared. There was an image of seven large light beings that seemed important for the cosmos and for humanity as if they were protectors and leaders. When I returned to my ordinary consciousness I felt like a bird that returned from endless space into its suffocating cage that was too small, and I literally gasped for breath. I was crestfallen and did not know what had happened to me. My heart reached out intensively to Jesus Christ. I tried to tell others about it, but continuously came up against resistance because they did not understand it and said it was a kind of delusion.

Caldana lay at approximately 600 metres altitude and from our house we could see Lake Maggiore. The beauty of the country and our surroundings, the artistic spirituality that you felt for these surroundings left a deep nostalgic image of beauty imprinted on me for the rest of my life. After I was in the Netherlands, I still had feelings of nostalgia for that old Italian villa with the turret for many years. A type of `akasha' had arisen there, an environment of inspiration, spirituality and beauty. Andries obviously did not experience life in this way. He led his own life and occupied himself with his work at Euratom and with his technical hobby, he collected all kinds of tools and in the space beside the kitchen he had set up a vast workshop.

At the beginning of the sixties of the previous century we were together with the other Europeans in Euratom, European pioneers, because the EEC had been set up, with only five Member States, a long time previous to that, in the fifties. This was the beginning of what would be a united Europa and our life was in fact new and full of promise. The region around Ispra was primitive and simple, but also picturesque and ethereal. Down through the years this has, of course, changed completely and has become very built up and materialistic. Speaking several languages with our English, French and German acquaintances, also Italian, helped me improve my skills and I enjoyed the contacts, free lifestyle in the picturesque surroundings, and could be brought to tears by the beauty of a shepherd with his herd of sheep on a solitary hillside in the Caldana countryside, with in the background the mountains and the sun setting above Lake Maggiore. I easily slipped into a fairy tale mood when, at noon, when Edwin had his afternoon nap, I wandered around the picturesque, Italian village and visited the villagers, who always received me warmly and with whom I could talk about everything and anything. What they told me concerning their lives reached far beyond me, but touched me in the sense that it concerned real life that was earthly, positive, strong and full of gentle sympathy. Some had, at that time, never been further than Milan, but they were wise and the conversations were instructive and interesting for me.

Presumably because my husband was a physicist, I became interested in the books of Albert Einstein (Mein Weltbild), astronomy and philosophy, Teilhard de Chardin etc. In Caldana I played records all day long, especially listening to the mass of Schubert and Mozart's concert in C. This music affected me very deeply and brought me to celestial heights. I enjoyed my son, but obviously, in spite of our well established Italian general practitioner, I could not prevent the Dutch paediatrician, who examined him in July 1964 in The Hague, from labelling him as a 'tropics child' who needed solid Dutch food. He was then three years old and had just got over the drama of breaking his leg. This happened at the Euratom crèche, where I had a temporary job. I then had to pay for the fact that I had to work against my will at Euratom. Andries had insisted on this, but I did not want to, because Edwin was still too small and I felt that I needed to be there for him. Under protest I accepted the job, but with resistance. It was a very nasty time. I therefore understand the observation of the paediatrician.

Then, in the sixties (1961-1964) my relationship with Andries deteriorated, we grew increasingly further apart from each other. He was, in his own way, crazy about Edwin. Although the situation at home was not easy, I managed that initially. I was rather passive about the problems, I accepted it, and Edwin and I wore three pullovers and two pairs of trousers in the wintertime in our ice-cold house, just to keep warm, the temperature was then 15 degrees. I was too young, too inexperienced, too naive, too innocent, too emotional, I took a stupid risk, I was not able to deal with Andries and was full of self-blame about him. He perhaps needed a mother more than a spouse, and I needed a father also more than a spouse in fact.

Our three-year stay in Caldana had been very important for me. I had the most important visions of my life there. Or perhaps they were just dreams or daydreams... I had premonitory dreams and received answers to spiritual questions. I wondered how spirits and ghosts were and then I dreamed that I was walking around in a French palace and encountered several men and women, in eighteenth century attire who did not notice my presence. It was said to me (by whom I do not know): `these people existed a couple of hundred years ago, and what you see now are `projections from the past', that applies to all apparitions of the deceased', therefore I should attach no importance to it. I found this explanation very interesting, because this subject was totally new to me. It reassured me, however, because I was frequently alone with Edwin in that large, detached villa, because Andries frequently made trips to America, to his parents, went on business trips to the Netherlands, to the head office in Brussels etc.

Then I `dreamed' I was in a faraway land in a mountainous region, and that I met a couple of men there who were sitting at a table at this place. It was no accidental meeting, they had something very strong and something very beautiful and very special. I seemed to know them and was vaguely aware that this was a very special visit, because for one of them I kneeled and bowed down respectfully. I do not know who that person was, but he was definitely very important. I appeared to know him. In another dream, or a vision between dreaming and waking perhaps, I met a very nice person, a man, who approached me and looked at me pleasantly. I saw his face clearly, he had a fairly long nose, not such a high forehead, dark and slightly round hairline and a slight beard. He looked at me affectionately with pale brown eyes. Then it was said (I do not know by whom): `this is: goodness, love and wisdom'.

The following morning, elated, I told Andries and my friends about my dream and this splendid man whom I had met that I had become amorous about. But as soon as I said it I realised that the words 'in love' were out of place here. It was something else, love on another, higher level, insofar as I could experience that then, at 26 years of age. In later years, after my familiarisation with the Theosophy and the Sufism, it all became much clearer to me.

These, and other, dreams and events in my life have proven to be a guiding principle, which gave me, in my later adventures and experiences in the spiritual and human area, a key to dealing with all kinds of situations. That key can be described as a deep, not always conscious faith in a higher Providence that at a given moment even exceeded confidence in the spiritual teachers whom I met. I knew that moments would always come, at which I would be able to 'see' or 'see through' certain truths and that exceeded the `knowing', or knowledge. Although I have always been grateful to them for specific knowledge that I received from them, I always went in my own direction, towards the unknown and unexpected.

Those three years in Italy have also been important for me on an artistic level and for having the possibility to inspire others. A couple of years later I received an invitation in the Netherlands from an old friend from Italy, Jan Aalte, for an exhibition of his paintings and those of his daughter, somewhere in the Netherlands, I think in Friesland. He wrote that thanks to being in Caldana with me, he had started to paint, and I had inspired him with my painter activities and example. Now father and daughter had reached the level that they exhibited their work together! I was very glad for them, but put the invitation aside, because I was busy with very different things. I was taking piano lessons in Milan at that time, from a concert pianist found by means of friends: an Italian, called Mozzati. I was already a rather good amateur, because since the age of ten I have had piano lessons.

Then something very unusual happened. I had a piano lesson in Milan, on a particular day in October 1963, approximately 50 km van Caldana, and I set off in my red Fiat 500 with my son. I would leave him with Italian friends, the family Molinari, during the lesson, as they were crazy about him. During my lesson it started to become foggy in Milan and in Italy it is possible that this can lead to inaccessible roads. When I had picked up my son and was getting into my car, it had become so terrible that I could not see my hand in front of my eyes. I wanted to get into my car and try nevertheless to get home that evening (approximately eight o'clock at night). What else could I do? I was not frightened, and nevertheless realised I that I would have to step in that car and leave, and that this was risky. Suddenly an unknown man emerged from the mist, he walked up to me and asked me where I had to go. I answered that I had to go in the direction of Varese to which he pleasantly replied: 'I must also go in that direction, follow behind me, then I will bring you to the 'autostrada'. I accepted his offer gladly and followed the rear lights of his car, beyond which I saw nothing due to the dense fog. At a given moment the fog abated and I recognised the way to the 'autostrada'. He stopped along the roadside, I waved gratefully to him and drove onto the motorway. I have frequently thought back to this, how this could happen, I sometimes seem nevertheless to be protected, because where did this man suddenly appear from? How did he know that I had a major problem due to the fog? It was at that moment a problem for Milanese as much as for thousands of others! During the same journey I also had considerable problems skidding on the wet, badly asphalted, mountain road of Caldana, but we managed to get through that. Supposedly thanks to my career on the carting track in Varese, where I learnt to skid and turn at high speed. But that day it seemed as if we were protected. Isn't that wonderful...

Approximately a year before I returned to the Netherlands, therefore in 1963, there was great excitement at Euratom that a skelter track had come to Varese and that it was very popular with the Euratomers and the Italians in the region. Of course we went to have a look. And at a certain moment, at the insistence of Andries and a friend, I took a seat in a skelter, although I was not really impressed by it all. That thing could drive at 120 km per hour and I was well instructed in advance by a man working there concerning technique. I drove away and before I knew it I was racing along the track. I was doing very well. I was ahead of everyone else and got good advice and instructions, during the races, by professional Italian drivers, who were there to promote and acquire publicity for certain large companies, and who instructed me with regard to how I could keep my competitors at bay, by among other things pressing my hot exhaust into their side! That exhaust was situated on the side of the skelter. As real Italians, however, those lads thought it was great that a young woman had chased everyone aside. Sometime later the championships were held in Varese, and who should have thought I would become champion. I got a beautiful medal and Andries was totally fed up, because after that time his colleagues teased him sometimes. The then Dutch director of Euratom, a professor whom Andries still knew from Delft, said to his companions when they encountered Andries: 'There goes the husband of Ms Alt...' I thought it was a good joke, but Andries did not.

On a certain day, at the beginning of 1963 if I remember correctly, I stood in the driveway of our villa and then an idea occurred to me, that these years of relative, rest inside and around me, would soon be over. It was as if I sensed suddenly that these three years would be a winding up of this period in my life and that turbulent times awaited me. I can remember that I just stood reflecting quietly and with conviction I said 'yes', I accepted it. Indeed I left on 4 July 1964 by plane with my son for the Netherlands and did not yet know that we would never return. One day I found a book about several spiritual trends in our bookcase, and read with great interest the pages about Crusaders, Freemasons, Sufi, Theosophers, Mormons, and other groups. Helena Petrovna Blavatsky, founder of the Theosophy movement, seemed to me quite soon to be a delightful person. I enjoyed her adventures, her rather wild youth, her miraculous contacts with spiritual masters in the Himalayas, her commitment to writing, partly, the books about Theosophy (secret teachings), her uprightness, dictated by her master. In the autumn of 1963 I decided to acquire some information at the Theosophical lodge in Amsterdam, found the address and received a quick reply, within three days no less (and that was incredibly quick at that time for our hamlet above the borough of Varese), from the Netherlands, with all kinds of data, concerning Theosophical lodges and libraries in Italy.

In July 1964 (American Independence Day nota bene) Edwin and I left for the Netherlands by plane (KLM tickets sent by my mother) and, after lengthy consultation with family, I started divorce proceedings, whereupon Andries submitted a counterclaim. Eventually we both got our divorce assigned, in which Andries was required to pay a modest amount of alimony for his son, with which I agreed. I went directly in search of a part-time job, so that I could be with my three-year-old son as much as possible and I succeeded! My life of independence could start! I was 27 years old. During the next few years in the Netherlands the spiritual inspiration, which I had experienced in Caldana, disappeared, probably due to the need to ensure that I could live independently, to look after my son as much as possible so that I could educate him and enable him to develop his unique qualities. Up to the age of forty-five I followed several training courses, such as bookkeeping, management and company law and eventually I became an accountant/administrator at a youth care agency. And I kept my languages alive as well: English, French, German, Italian and later some Russian.

* * *

Chapter 3. 1965 – 1975. In Holland. Theosophy. Astrology

I have done much reflection concerning the capricious inversions of fate. I have determined that I have in fact never been a `victim' of circumstances, but have always taken responsibility, because I made the choices myself. It means that you interpret what happens and decide for yourself if and how to react. Therefore no lamenting is necessary afterwards. Krishnamurti said: `Never react'. I notice every time how true this is and how useful the character training is, as a result of the self-discipline acquired due to not reacting, and especially the growing wisdom! It is undeserved to blame yourself or others later. Perhaps this sounds rather `harsh', but if I want to live consciously, this fact must be borne in mind. Of course this also means that you must develop self-knowledge, and that you must learn not to always `give in' or `agree'. Furthermore, there is a time for everything, the correct time, and in that sense we follow the easiest course, like a flowing river. The course of the river always arranges the `correct moment'. We always have our free will, and we use this whenever we choose the 'how'. In the context of this development of the character I always try to live in a conscious and creative manner and not fall back on the bleak aspects of pessimism, regrets, debt and dejection. But that was not at all easy...

When I arrived on 4 July 1964 in the Netherlands, I picked up a telephone directory to look up the Theosophical association and saw a name: D.J.P. Kork and a phone number. I rang immediately. Thus I came upon the Theosophical organization, of which Mr Kork was the leader. I attended the lectures about Theosophy and was delighted at what I heard. He interpreted the Theosophical studies and I knew straight away : `Yes, this is true, this is absolutely true!' I heard about planetary revolutions and races, about the major religions of the world, about the philosophy of `No religion higher than Truth', about karma and reincarnation, about India and the Masters of Wisdom, about the Masters who by means of H.P. Blavatsky had introduced Theosophy to the world: Morya and Koot Hoomi, concerning the sevenfold composition of a human being, and the distinction between the mortal part and the immortal part, concerning exoteric and esoteric (the inner and external side of the religions), concerning the difference between the path of the left hand and the path of the right hand, all this was of priceless value to me. It gave me the key to developing my capacity for understanding, and I learned how important that is, it is the most important (!) condition for spiritual development. I never missed a lecture by Mr Kork. I learnt about oriental religions, about life and death, mystery schools, initiation in the mysteries, the universal brotherhood of humanity, the mental evolution of mankind ('the temple of the Lord is not made by hand and no sound is heard') and cosmos, concerning Theosophy and occultism and esoteric Christianity and a lot of other matters. I became acquainted with secret teachings. In a Theosophical studies club in Amsterdam we received a 'roadmap' for reading this impressive book. Under no circumstances must it be read in the normal order, but in certain order of chapters and subject, crisscross throughout the book, then you will perhaps understand something of it and have an overview. The teachings were a revelation for me, and from the very first lecture by Mr Kork I knew that I had come 'home'. I was attracted by the knowledge and it even appeared familiar to me. The pieces of the puzzle fell into place and my hunger for knowledge was satisfied. I cultivated pleasant, personal contacts in the organization, and my male and female friends helped me through the difficult and uncertain time during my divorce. It was a traumatic time, because my spouse used every weapon he could against me, due to the fact that he assumed I wanted to strip him financially. An unfounded fear, as was later proven and that he, if he had known me better, could have known. He showed some sadism at times. For me, as a naive twenty-something, it was all very terrifying. Mr Kork knew however in advance exactly how this situation would develop and he assured me that the outcome would not be to my disadvantage, and he proved to be right about this. People have supported me greatly, and for that I will always be grateful.

In 1964, I became an official member of a Theosophical organisation, or to put it correctly: the Theosophical Society Point Loma, California, and I became friendly with Mr Kork and his wife. Because of my background and experience I rapidly became a member of the governing board of the lodge in The Hague and I gladly helped him set up his written courses (`Thinking differently', `the Big Misunderstanding', `the jewels of Wisdom'), which are now still used by the Theosophical organization. In hindsight my meeting with Mr Kork was very meaningful. I was still too young and too ignorant of esoteric matters to realise that he was my `spiritual teacher'. He was recommended by his predecessor, William Hartley, who designated him as his successor, in other words as international leader of the Theosophical Society Point Loma. Kork was a youthfully optimistic, fairly inconspicuous, almost colourless man of fifty with penetrating eyes. He worked as a civil servant at the municipality in The Hague. My mother found him rather dull, with which I did not agree at all, because of his knowledge of Theosophy and his lectures were impressive and he supplied me with spiritual nourishment, for which I longed. He could understand the difficult Theosophical teachings and translate these into easily understandable language and, as a result, it was for most people not only knowledge, but also a kind of `character', that he transferred. That character was gentle and pleasant. He had a great sense of humour. In that time I accompanied him, along with some others, sometimes on a tour through the cities in Germany and the Netherlands, to hold lectures there in Theosophical lodges and in this way to establish more of a reputation for Theosophy. He invited me to go along because he wanted to present me to a number of people and to introduce me as an up-and-coming woman of Theosophy who had a promising future in the discipline. He expected much of me and this has often happened in the course of my life at esoteric gatherings. If I noticed this, I withdrew directly into myself, because I did not consider myself able to satisfy those expectations. It was inevitable, that we developed too much of a personal bond and that conflicts were never far away. It did not take long for me to conclude that I had to adjust my ideals with respect to people, and I had to 'return to myself'. This came with considerable disillusionment.

At the end of 1965, after the divorce was pronounced final in The Hague, Andries proposed that we nevertheless still try for a year. I wanted that possibility as we were still nevertheless a family and I still cared for him. At that time he worked at Euratom in Brussels, and thereby we moved at the beginning of 1966 to a beautiful condominium in the district Audergem in Brussels. When I returned to The Hague in September 1966, because the experiment in Brussels offered no development possibilities, I still continued my involvement in the organization for some time. At that time, encouraged by Mr Kok, I wrote a couple of articles in the bi-monthly magazine, Theosophical Life. In March 1967, when I was 30 years old, my first article was then published, entitled: 'Ideas of someone who has studied Theosophy'. In this I philosophised, in a rather headstrong manner, concerning the theory and practice of Theosophical teachings, concerning the danger of dogmatism, arrogance and naivety, concerning the deep meaning which had been attached to Theosophical knowledge and subtlety, where the wisdom of everyday life, also sometimes called 'common sense', seems to have been overlooked. I believed that true Theosophy had not been intended for those who were starved of intellectual knowledge, the 'curious ones', the consumers of books, but for those who sought the true spiritual life, who were prepared to make the effort to 'become', and eventually to 'be'. An 'inner school' therefore: to obtain the knowledge about and of themselves and the cosmos, and put into practice this knowledge, it is a struggle, it is the quantum leap to a new consciousness, a new form of being. The perspective of Theosophy was raising the consciousness to Budhi level (Buddhism is not meant here), to the level of the Christ consciousness. Theosophy is considered as the synthesis of religion, science and is certainly not purely academically intended. Mr Kork could convey this very well and he helped many people in their spiritual growth.

A year later my article entitled 'Belief, Knowledge and Truth' was published, concerning the inner awakening of people and the path in search of God. It also concerned the dangers and pitfalls they encountered, concerning the need to display the capacity to understand distinctions and to possess inner strength. I concluded that truth must be understood as that pure crystal, which sets us in motion from within, which leads us to our quest and which is difficult to imagine. I indicated that this Truth, which drives us in this search, is the image of Perfection, of God, a picture that we keep deep in our hearts, where we intuitively presume something, but which is difficult to be consciously aware of just the same. I indicated that this can only be found in my opinion by means of the human being in his/her entirety and not by his or her separate aspects, such as that of thinking and feeling. With people in their entirety I mean: in what they think, do and are, and I referred to the path of Jesus Christ that leads to the objective. This path was, in my opinion, the growth from an unconscious faith to a conscious faith, to a state of being, to a unity with God. Years later, I would become acquainted with the mystic 'inner school' of Sufi Inayat Khan, which would bring me still further along the inner path.

In 1965, I followed a very inspiring course in astrophysics in The Hague at the planetarium that was then still in existence. During the lectures, accompanied by splendid music, the starry sky revolved above our heads, and one could clearly see the positions of the constellations, and (for me) the mystic environment of the cosmos with the galaxy and other astral schemes, and I had the desire to separate from the planet and soar up in the cosmos. I also started a written course in astrology at the Pelman Institute in Leiden and kept myself occupied with that for a couple of years. My teacher complimented me for the way in which I 'clarified' the relationships of the planets and that stimulated me. He indicated that this is the most important and most difficult part of astrology. Later I had much pleasure from having this basic knowledge of astrology, and I complemented my knowledge regularly with incidental courses and workshops. I obtained more insight into others and also myself. I have however never felt the need to draw up the horoscope of others, which I preferred to leave to 'professional' astrologers. I learnt from Mr Kosman, my professor, who was known to be a good astrologer, that one must undergo an inner education of realisation, and that one must be a serious astrologer for at least fifty years to be able to be called an 'astrologer', in the true sense of the word. He admitted that this requires a growth in character, a growth to inner adulthood. 'Superficial' people, mainly in the sense of life in relation to social and cultural life, can never penetrate the deep knowledge of astrology, the important way of 'clarifying' the planetary relationships.

I was active for approximately four years in the Theosophical organization and I spent that time studying, working for the governing board and in discussion groups. In ordinary, 'secular', life I had found a part-time job as a bookkeeper, so that I could remain at home with my son. My mother supported me and was always prepared to mind him. I became a member of a tennis club, where I met my second spouse, Herbert, a year later. I knew that Mr Kork hoped that I would entirely dedicate myself to working for Theosophy, because he had determined that I had connections with the spiritual masters of Theosophy. Due to all kinds of developments and entanglements in my life however, I became less and less involved in the activities in and around the organization. I grew away from it, because I wanted to go out, play tennis, meet nice men, lie on the beach, buy nice clothing, earn my own money etc. I felt trapped, feeling that a spiritual involvement was expected of me, for which I was not yet ready. Furthermore, I had my practical, daily obligations and was responsible for the education of my son.

A couple of years ago, around 2006, I was told something very educational by a good astrologer, he was called Patrick van Haag. He had concluded from my horoscope that I had done much for humanity, in my previous incarnation, as part of a task I was given. In my current incarnation spiritual knowledge had to come from me, I had to work on my own realisation of consciousness and no longer spread the message of others. After a period of painful misunderstandings and inevitable events, I said a final farewell to the organization, but not to Theosophy, in 1970! The familiarisation with Theosophy would be very important during my future life. It provided insight into the composition of the cosmos and humanity, I became acquainted with the universal laws which underpin everything, and the mystic aspect (William Quan Judge: `Seek within',

'Know Thyself') would always help me in finding and following 'the right' direction. In the seventies a totally new era dawned. Mr Kork would have said: 'Maria retreats into obscurity' (with regard to spirituality) and I led a pleasant and sport-loving life with my boyfriend, Herbert, who in April 1973 became my second husband. He moved in with me, he was eleven years younger and he did not know what to do with his life. He had just come out of service and had a lot of problems with painful lumps on his fingers and a couple of other ailments, such as hay fever. He played guitar and I accompanied him on the piano. We played songs from Simon and Garfunkel, and he brought this to the TROS television channel talent show together with a friend, in which they sang songs they composed with guitar accompaniment. They came second, after Tineke Schouten, a well-known cabaret performer nowadays. I was content to build a life with him, for us to develop ourselves, to learn and to experience. A younger man has always proven for me to be the most 'bearable' choice. The relations between my son and Herbert had not always been the best and there was much quarrelling. They were obviously jealous of each other and I had to call them into line regularly one after the other. Their age difference was 13 years. After the separation of Herbert and I in 1989, sixteen years later, they became good friends and they still are. I admit that my son, because of his own father, Andries, has not had much pleasure in life, but instead, however, has had much sorrow and frustration. Herbert was a good tennis player and together we won quite a few prizes and trophies, but that due to his top form, not my tennis qualities, because I was certainly no expert. We made major trips twice a year, travelling to Morocco, Greece, United Kingdom, Scotland etc. and we went regularly on winter sport holidays together.

* * *

Chapter 4. 1975 – 1983. The Findhorn Community in Scotland. Anthroposophy. Gurdjieff

I had, from a spiritual point of view, indeed spent time 'in obscurity'. In 1975, and 1976, on my initiative, Herbert and I visited the well-known commune Findhorn Foundation in Scotland, in Inverness. We met Peter and Eileen Caddy there, the founders of the commune, who have become famous because of their spiritual manner of life and spiritually based practice of agriculture and horticulture. Their contact and relationship with nature had for example produced a giant cabbage, which had received rather a lot of publicity within and outside the United Kingdom. They told us that they received teachings from a spiritual being called Limitless Love and Truth, about which the American New Age writer David Spangler wrote a number of books such as: 'Revelation: the Birth of a New Age'. He wrote about the birth of a new era, which would distinguish itself by the expanding consciousness of humanity. He addressed in particular the Western Christian people, who would be enabled by means of a new vision to create a new world based on spirituality and universal brotherhood. By means of meditative training and renewed thinking he would come in contact with the higher worlds. These higher worlds are areas of awareness with a different vibration, as a result of which they are invisible to our five senses and the earthly consciousness. This contact superceded the former 'mediumship' and creates mediators, interpreters of higher knowledge, which will not be experienced as if it is coming from a source outside ourselves, but from our own thinking and from our own heart. David Spangler demonstrates that in this new era people will look less and less for guides/ outside of themselves, but that they will discover that the spiritual world cooperates with us by means of our own thinking, our own imagination and our intuition. The new era at the beginning of the seventies heralded the esoteric 'hot topic' and proclaimed the cosmic Christ and the return of Christ. We met dozens of people of several nationalities in Findhorn, and we learned much from our contact with them. They radiated fun, gentleness, joy, intelligence and candidness. You could communicate very amiably with them and life was easy, happy and spiritual. They practised concentrating their consciousness, as they called, their Higher Self. I thought that this meant their soul. Continuing our travels through Scotland, we stayed there for a week both times. Herbert enjoyed Findhorn, however, he was less interested in the esoteric aspects than in the nice young girls. Well, that was OK with me...

In the seventies I also looked up the anthroposophers and became acquainted with eurhythmics. I took part in a course and experienced what these movements do with soul and spirit. I thought it was splendid, as well as the lectures and other activities in their centre. But already I found it all rather cerebral and was reading books at home by Rudolf Steiner, particularly concerning the attainment of consciousness of the higher worlds. I visited a study group for a short time in a living room on the Carel van Bylandtlaan, where a certain engineer called Ekkers had just started spreading the teachings of Gurdjieff. I can still remember that he told us one evening what an incredible eye opener it had been, that then he realised `that people, in fact, have nothing to do with, and are therefore completely separate from, the actions and responses of others, because that is exclusively the responsibility of the other'. You can just ignore such a reaction and not take it personally, it need cause you no pain. I thought of Krishnamurti's words: `Don't react'. Ekkers said that this insight had been an enormous relief and release for him, and he had therefore no longer related to the negativity of another or felt guilty. In our group someone muttered something like "inevitable", yet in my opinion this is an unreasonable, typically Calvinistic awareness of guilt. Ekkers resolutely rejected this weak counter argument however. I found those study evenings very interesting, but in the long run there was something too heavily philosophical in them for me. I obviously did not yet need Gurdjieff. That would change in the future, in 1992, when I met the 'three Russians'. More about this later.

* * *

CHAPTER 5. 1983 – 1989. TOUR THROUGH THE SACRED PLACES OF INDIA. FIRST CONTACT WITH THE SUFISM OF HAZRAT INAYAT KHAN. AURA- AND CHAKRA HEALING. THE DANCING DERVISHES IN KONYA, TURKEY

In 1983 and 1984 I followed a two-year course in auras and chakra healing, whereby Herbert, my spouse, had major problems, 'because', he found, 'with this training we are growing away from each other'. He had the feeling that this development would destroy our life together. In that training I would learn how to use my energy and that was indeed serious. His intuition appeared correct. A friend at my work, Peter Eberhardt, visited us at that time, with his girlfriend Roseanne, to try to quell Herbert's protests. However, that worked so well that Herbert moved in with Roseanne a couple of years later, in 1989, and they married. He had seen the light indeed! It was already not going well for a couple of years between Herbert and I, we had grown apart. Our life had mainly consisted of sport, travel, our practical development and study. That was all okay. He had always followed a number of training courses, such as human resources and management, and became increasingly self-assured. He started to make a career for himself and was now staff manager at Akzo. The communication between us worsened: there was less and less understanding and allegiance to each other, but a lot of irritation. I already wanted to separate in the mid-eighties, but because he didn't want that then I knew that I had be careful, because he would carry out his threat and clean me out. I also had a good job myself. I decided to leave the matter to destiny, to karma, and quietly wait. Otherwise a tough legal battle awaited me. This was because, just like Andries, he was obsessed with money and was rather miserly. Destiny solved this situation splendidly: Roseanne visited him at his office and told him what she thought of him and he went to ground. He thus left me as a well-to-do man (savings account, country house in Friesland, garage), shouting from the staircase 'that I would not get a penny from him'. However, this was no problem, I would have my own work and income.

Meanwhile I was homesick for India, for the Theosophy and the spirituality of the Far East. In 1983, I attended a reading of Sufi Pir Waseem Khan, the eldest son of the Sufi master Hazrat Inayat Khan, and he made a major impact on me. He made a very erudite impression, spoke sixteen languages, scattered inspiring Sufi teachings as manna as far as we were concerned and, although he was spiritual head of the Sufi order, he also gave a practical impression of a businessman. I thought literally: 'this is what I also want to be'. Then I heard accidentally that the Sufi group would make a three-week trip around India and visit various places of pilgrimage of several religions. I rang the headquarters in The Hague and asked if could join this trip, in spite of the fact that I was not a member of the Sufi group. I was invited for a conversation with the tour leader Amid Kort, and afterwards Herbert and I could take part in this trip. At the beginning of 1984 we left with about thirty Sufi: Dutch, English and Norwegians, as far as I can remember. Amid was a fantastic tour leader and from New Delhi he brought us to Agra, where the Taj Mahal stands, Bodh Gaya, where I sat under the Bodhi tree, where Gautama the Buddha became enlightened, Rishikesh to the river Ganges, the sacred place of the yogi, Katmandu with its special temples, in New Delhi we visited among other things the house where Inayat Khan lived and died, and a lot of other sacred places.

We suffered a lot of deprivations while travelling, became sick, meditated and talked with each other. He knew a great deal about those places and concerning Indian cultures. I remember that this trip was a fantastic experience for me, yet not for Herbert, because he was constantly sick.

After this trip, on a return journey, thirty years after I had left high school, I met the then director of my school: Ms Prins. Amid had told me about her, and also that she had been the wife of the youngest brother of Inayat Khan. He was called Muzaffar Khan. She was now murshida, a spiritual teacher of the Sufi Circle. I greeted her very timidly, because I knew that I had not behaved in an exemplary fashion at high school. I said to her that I was still ashamed about that but she laughed and answered that it had not been really so terrible. She invited me for a chat. That conversation had to take place later, because I was busy with a course in auras and chakra healing, and there were all kinds of matters that occupied me, so I did not come to visit her in the short term.

I discovered the training course 'Intuitive Development', also called 'auras and chakra healing', which would take two years, the first year in The Hague and the second year in Utrecht. My teachers, Maggy Wishaupt and Martin McCuskey, had studied at the Berkeley Psychic Institute in California. 'Intuitive' was intended to mean examining one's own energy in the aura and the functioning of the chakras. I was interested in this, because I wanted to discover how I functioned as a person, how my energy worked in daily life and in interactions with others, by which forces I operated. Could I indeed heal other people? How could I find true freedom?

We had a lesson every two weeks and had in the meantime practical exercises to do, because that was what it would all be about eventually: how do I 'feel and see' and how do I put it into practice? Training in the first year had been aimed at (self) help and (self) healing. Developing 'psychic' powers was no aim in itself, yet it could emerge as a consequence of a natural, spiritual development. 'Being psychic' was not considered to be something special, more as the result of cleansing and refining both the inner and external senses. The aim of the course was to gain insight by learning how we can free ourselves of limitations and conditioning, which impedes us from 'clearly seeing', and to become ourselves. We learnt to free ourselves from the psychological dominance of other people, ideologies etc. We are mostly unaware of this dominance, and if you pay close attention you will notice that there are very few people who can really 'stand their ground'. Most people are manipulated by their surroundings without minding too much about this, because they do not, in fact, know who they really are. We obtained valuable insight into what makes people who they are, the energy field through and around us, and how to purify it. We learnt from within the colours of the aura and how to see the chakra both of ourselves and of others, and I succeeded in this if I closed my eyes slightly. I found it funny that, before the exercise started, in order to tune ourselves in an astral 'fan of colours' was 'thrown' into the group and I could see it from within quite clearly if I closed my eyes. It looked like the colour palette for painting. We were given exercises in visualisation and imagination, to feel and to sense from within the radiance of others, also of plants, trees and animals with the energy of our hands. We learnt the function and experienced the meaning of chakras. Halfway through the course I just stopped, because it seemed old fears had returned. I did not know if that was to do with the exercises of the course. After a phone call with the course leader, Maggy, I went to Utrecht a short while later. She put me at ease that these symptoms would disappear if I learnt to manage my energy well by letting the energies flow through my body.

Then something interesting happened. Just before the end of the course I had done the meditation exercises at home, early in the afternoon, and was on my way to my work, on the Sweelinckplein in The Hague. I walked along the Frederik Hendriklaan to my work and suddenly I had the feeling that my spirit was focused, that I could intensely observe everything and when I looked at people on the street I noticed that I could see right through them, with a feeling of love. I found all these people to be very beautiful. I thought: `If only people knew how splendid they are, then they would not look so sombre in this way...' It was a special, inner state and when I arrived, a little further up the street almost at my work, I thought: `I must tell this to Ms Prins and ask her what is going on with me, what does this experience mean... And suddenly a lady appeared on my left from a side street, she started walking just ahead of me, about three metres ahead. I saw in utter disbelief that it was Ms Prins. I thought: `What a strange coincidence' and I walked up and tapped her on the shoulder. She looked at me and I greeted her and told her that I had thought of her exactly at that moment and how astonished I was to see her, as I was just thinking that I would like to discuss an important subject with her. I told her there and then, on the street, what I had experienced. Had I suddenly become clairvoyant? She laughed a little and reacted as if my experience was the most normal thing in the world. I then became calmer and she said: `That was your heart chakra which opened up, but now you must come and visit me very soon nevertheless. I live here, on the corner of the Banstraat'. We continued on further to my work and I told her about the course in auras and chakra healing and that I wanted to finish it before I came to see her. It was just a couple months. But she was not in agreement at all, to my amazement. She indicated that I should stop with that course, because it would only do damage. But I continued obstinately, as always, in my decision to finish the course.

A couple of weeks later I visited her; there was also a Norwegian Sufi present, whom I knew from the India trip. A very nice, sensitive man. We went to sit at his table, the three of us, and I told them about my aura and chakra course, and I did so with great enthusiasm. Yet my tone became less and less buoyant, as I saw to my amazement that they were not at all pleased with my tale. I tried to be even more precise, because I thought, `it cannot be possible that they are angered by this?' It was not so awful, but I was admonished and warned about the spiritual dangers I was exposed to on this course and that I should stop as soon as possible. They said that I was forcing my psyche, and that this could have major repercussions. And furthermore that the Sufism teaches that these developments happened gradually, by means of meditation, a pure manner of acting and studying the teachings of Inayat Khan, and that I could damage myself by following this course. I listened in disappointment, but nevertheless stated firmly that I wanted to finish the course because, if I started something, I always finished it. The conversation continued for a while and then I went home. They for sure found me to be obstinate and extremely determined. I did indeed finish that course and later gave lectures about it at the Freemasons and the Theosophists. I did not have the impression that the course had damaged me at all. I have always been careful and did not put myself in unknown or risky situations or circumstances. You can somehow sense such a risk, however, and then it is up to yourself to decide if you want take such a risk. So not me.

At the end of 1985, in mid- December, we briefly went with a group of Sufi, under the guidance of Sufi Amid, on a tour of Turkey. The ultimate destination was Konya, where we would attend the birthday of Rumi, the ceremonies of the dancing Dervishes, on 17 December. At that time these ceremonies had not yet been commercialised and it was generally real spiritual masters who carried out the ceremonies. The ceremonies were seemingly permitted by the Turkish government, who turned a blind eye, but for a long time the Dervishes had lived 'underground', as inconspicuously as possible, and had worked as shoe-makers, tailors, etc. My spouse Herbert also went along on this trip, although not entirely enthusiastically, because he did not have much interest in spiritual matters. That was something he unfortunately made clear, both to me and to the others in the group.

One of the most the splendid experiences, at the beginning of the trip to Turkey, was the visit to Izmir and Ephesia, the place where Mary, the mother of Jesus, was looked after by the apostle John during her last few years. Recently Pope Benedict XVI, during his official visit to Turkey, paid a visit to this. It lies on top of the mountain and is a very sacred place. You can feel this in the atmosphere. There is a small, restored house with an altar dedicated to Mary, and if you go inside and reflect, you experience a golden feeling as if your aura is elevated. This location is a place of pilgrimage for Christians and Muslims and has meanwhile been visited by three popes. The atmosphere is nourishing and mesmerising and I could have spent hours in meditation there. The sepulchre of the apostle John is also in Ephesia.

On arriving in Konya, we found in our hotel (a modern skyscraper) a large, varied companionship of Orientals and Occidentals! The environment in the busy reception hall of the hotel had something very special: open, warm and dynamic. There was the kind of solidarity found in a large international brotherhood and everyone spoke to everyone else, known or unknown, and appointments were made concerning where and by whom zikrs would be held the following evening. Zikrs are mystic Sufi-exercises, during the singing of eulogies to Allah, where the practitioners reach a state of ecstasy and experience a feeling of nostalgia for the divine. This feeling of nostalgia is characteristic and can develop into a tangible contact with Allah, with God. The Sufi consider this experience as the aim of the exercise. For the dancing ceremonies we went on the evening of the Rumi anniversary, 17 December 1985, to a large sport hall, the Ataturk hall, which was full of people and black with cigarette smoke. I wondered how the dancing dervishes could breathe and move in this atmosphere. After speeches by a number of Turkish dignitaries, among them ministers and the mayor, the music started. A dervish in a long, black gown and high camel-hair fez on his head played quiet, intensely melancholic music on a tiny violin. Entirely absorbed in his art, apart from his surroundings, whereas the room became even smokier and more rambunctious.

Afterwards a splendid concert followed on string, percussion and wind instruments, where a blind singer sang a type of hymn in a very imposing manner. After the pause the dancing ceremonies started. It became somewhat quieter in the sports hall, then a row of dervishes with black gowns and high fez on their heads, preceded by the sheikh, a slight small man with an affectionate manner, quietly entered. This was an essential moment of love, which radiated to all people present. The dervishes moved in a worthy, devoted manner, there was a serious expression on their faces and their attention was turned inside. There was an air of peace about them. The orchestra played and the blind singer sang a prayer. A large male choir accompanied him. Then slowly the dancing began, a slow vorticity developed, aristocratically and gracefully. The vorticity became faster and the twirling, white robes billowed up, showing a pattern in choreography. What was played out became the order of the cosmos, the planet scheme with the sun and the twirling planets before it, the entity of all parts of the cosmos, which originates from the same Being and is part of the one God. There was the message, that people had apparently turned away from God, but that they will return to Him as a result of inner growth. Twelve sheikhs in long, white robes whirled round, and a sheikh in a black robe, elegantly and with dignity and devotion turning around, with a deep inner perception, like the twelve planets that revolved around the sun. The thirteenth sheikh, dressed in black, made sure they did not go into a trance, because that was not the intention. The raised right hand ensured that the divine energy was channelled via the downward pointing left hand to humanity, as an aid to reaching the divine.

Afterwards we were invited to the home of one of the dervishes. There a group of about ten people sat on the ground in a circle and practised singing wasiva's and the zikr intensively. There was tremendous energy in the chamber. I took part in the zikr and I had the feeling that I opened up, in a devoted manner, like a flower. I saw a flower in my spirit, light pink, a young tulip (to my amazement no rose!) appearing with a beautiful, straight light green stem and slightly upward pointing leaves, not limply hanging down. There was a light, tingling environment around this. I felt happy and light. This was an enigmatic experience. Years later I came to know that this tulip, literally as I have described it, is considered in Turkish Islam as a symbol of the properties of God, of Allah, the property of beauty. I saw an image of a special painting technique (I think that this is called buru), a technique where much water is used and the paint is allowed to run and spreads itself, in a blue marbled effect with, in the foreground, the tulip I had seen, literally as it appeared in my vision. I heard later that our Dutch tulips indeed initially originated in Turkey...

At last I decided to join the Sufi group and on 12 June 1986 I was initiated by Murshida, Ms Sharifa Prins, as Sufi and Mureed (student) of Inayat Khan. The spiritual connection was established by the great Sufi musician, poet and mystic, Murshid Hazrat Inayat Khan, the founder of the Sufi Circle. Now that I write this down, I suddenly feel the inspiring and loving connection with Murshid, after more than thirteen years of distance, in the midst of turbulence, a succession of events in my life, complications with members of the Sufi Circle, unjust accusations, attacks which I had to endure because I did what I thought was right, but with which the Sufi leaders were obviously not in agreement. But more about this later. Now that connection with Murshid brings me into that light, golden, inner state, in which I experience space, promise, inspiration and creativity. I feel my soul dance, the 'dancing soul', such as Murshid called it. The brilliance and the glow of the spiritual light: 'Your music makes my soul dance', such as Inayat Khan expressed himself in his writings, the obligation of mystic and music. Is that the environment in which Murshid now finds himself? How was it then that that door closed at a certain moment, from approximately 1992 onwards, and totally changed my life? I had left the path of Murshid and had gone astray? Or I had broadened my path by seeking new experiences. I tend to think so. My life has been tempestuous ever since.

It started with difficulties in 1989: in my work, my divorce after the first Indian trip in 1989, difficulties with the Sufi leaders, because I found that I was treated impolitely at my initiation to cheraga (cherag: bringer of light and official at the ceremonies of the Sufi Universal Service of Worship). Due to all the problems I drank too much alcohol, especially when I came home from work. In February 1991 I had an accident on the street, the result being a shattered ankle, which was restored by means of an operation by the surgeons with plates and screws. I was laid up for eight months as a result. Then, after a letter of complaint from me to Haseem Khan, the leader of the Sufi group and the youngest son of Inayat Khan, concerning the way in which I was treated at my initiation to cheraga, my initiation to cheraga nevertheless still followed on 5 July 1991 (the birthday of Inayat Khan). I was initiated by Murshid Haseem, with my murshida, Ms Prins, at her house. At this initiation I received a new name: firstly was called I Rani (queen) and that now changed to Maharani (great queen). I felt rather uncomfortable there. This new name meant that I had to grow into the task from being an earthly queen to a queen of a higher, spiritual, order. I was a little scared of that name, because I thought that there would, however, be problems with my colleague Sufi and I found it a little 'too' much of a good thing. I still remarked that a maharani belonged to a maharadja, and that I would thus eventually find one. Both gave me the advice and the assignment on this special occasion to learn, not to take any notice of jealousy around me, and if others were jealous of me that I should let this run off me like drops of water on my raincoat. They were both so friendly and warm, I was very happy with my initiation to cheraga. If I think about it, I must admit that I was no easy student (mureed). I think that the major changes in my life, such as the difficulties at work and during my divorce, as well as other complications, had sent my nervous system out of balance. I was still far removed from the `foundations of adulthood'. By `foundations' I mean the firm rootedness, the ability to relativise, in the first place in relation to oneself. I would have to live several years longer and become somewhat older, before this began to sink in. My need for freedom and finding my own inner responsibility, my own `being', would gradually begin to shine however.

Hazrat Inayat Khan, the founder of the international Sufi Movement, was born in India, in Baroda, and lived from 1882 to 1927. He preached a universal message of spiritual freedom, of religious ideals, of respect for all religions, prophets and religious books. I cite the Sufi monthly magazine: `His message is to unite daily life and religion with each other so that every action can be carried by the spirit and can be fruitful: a manner of living interwoven with timeless mysticism. Sufism is characterised by a positive and constructive attitude to life, based on striving towards a notion of brotherhood. Inayat Khan wanted to build a bridge between East and West, and from his literature it is clear that he was also focused on Christ, although he was originally an Indian Moslem. But in the immenseness of India the dividing line between Moslems, Hindus, Sikhs, Buddhists, Christians and others has frequently been much less pronounced than in the west and has had much reciprocal influence, and there is generally a great deal of tolerance in daily life. Inayat Khan was a great musician and played on the vina. He was called the Beethoven of India. As Sufi he belonged the line of Moiniddin Chisti and to the order of the Sufi musicians. In 1989 with a Hindu girlfriend I visited the tomb and the dargah of Moiniddin Chisti in Ajmer, Rajasthan, about three hundred kilometres south of New Delhi. That was a marvellous trip. In New Delhi we caught the local `high speed bus' to Ajmer. The bus was packed and in the back ten picturesque and brightly-clothed women were sitting. During the trip they started to sing suddenly in harmony, and specifically songs from their culture. I found it splendid and the several hours journey became an inspiring event. `High speed buses' in India are exciting, those who have visited India can imagine this: a virtuoso driver who presses hard on the accelerator, constantly honking the horn, cyclists riding askew, people and animals, and for me the wonder that I survived. On the way we had to change to another bus. We stood out among all those Indians: a Hindu woman wrapped in sari with a dot on her forehead and a tall blonde European woman in Indian clothing. To buy tickets we had to stand in line at the counter, but just before it was our turn there were no more tickets left. That was not so nice and we looked at each other wide-eyed. What should we do now? But suddenly a man appeared from among the bystanders, who were all staring at us, with two bus tickets to the place we were going in his outstretched hand. He said in Hindi, 'You take these, I do not need them'. That was a real miracle and we gratefully made use of his offer. He did not even want money. We continued our trip and arrived at the tomb of the great artist and saint: Moiniddin Chisti. The large mosque was full people, men in white with their forehead on the ground praying, separate compartments with praying women, veiled and also in white. We were not veiled and not in white clothing, but nobody bothered us. We passed through to the central section, the tomb of Chisti. We were permitted to come close and to touch the chord surrounding the sepulchre. On the four corners of the tomb sat Agni priests who performed a fire ceremony and to whom we gave some money. We bowed our heads in devotion standing before them, sent up a prayer to this master of Indian music and I held the chord with both hands. At a given moment I felt such an enormous surge of energy around me and passing through me that the chord I held in my hands started to tremble and shake like an electric current passed through it. It seemed as if my kundalini was aroused. It was impressive and inspiring. I understood that I was in a very special place, and that I was receiving a kind of initiation of fire. Later I realised that this visit had intervened in my life in an almost raw and basic manner, because since my return to the Netherlands, which was thus in February 1989, it seemed my life was completely shaken up, perhaps to free me from the 'untruth'...

Since my return to the Netherlands a lot happened and that lasted for about six years.

In the dargah we walked back between the mob of praying men and, in separate areas, past the women and we received of course the usual looks. I suddenly felt less relaxed, realising that in this time in the Moslem world a curse had been pronounced on Salmon Rushdie concerning his book 'The Satanic Verses'.

I hoped that someone would not stand up and confront us. In these times of growing tension we made our way slowly to the exit and then as we turned around for a final farewell to this inspiring spot, we found ourselves confronted by an Indian soldier, who had always accompanied us without our having noticed it, for our security. He greeted us, turned around and walked away. We greeted him, greatly impressed, and returned by 'high speed bus' to New Delhi. The return trip ran smoothly and now that I think about it I still think to myself: 'man, that bus was so dangerous'. But the drivers, who drove like crazy on those immense, dead straight and narrow Indian roads, filled with bustling people, cows, cars and much more in order to make their trip on time, sat deep in their 'hara' (the inner balance, which is located in the lower belly region) that we arrived unharmed. Something like I have also experienced in Nepal, when we went by bus on a narrow mountain road full of breaches and holes with on one side an abyss of hundreds of meters, to a temple on the top of a mountain. A couple of women from the group started screaming, but I sat beside the driver and then I felt his good judgement and knew that no errors would be made, however he steered.

I was active in the Sufi group for seven years. I, as hard-working service provider, was a member of two governing boards, of the temple in Katwijk and the Banstraat centre, followed lectures and classes, did exercises and was very involved in the message of love, harmony and beauty of Inayat Khan. I was a dedicated Sufi. Twice, in 1989, and 1990, I visited Dargah in New Delhi (the tomb of Inayat Khan) and travelled around in India.

Dargah was an island of peace and beauty, in the middle of Delhi. Opposite Dargah was a slum, built up from crates from the rubbish tip, where the very poor lived in dark, dingy huts. There were hundreds of them. There were regular food distributions from the Dargah, and there was a little school, which was financed by the Sufi. The activities of the Dargah were conducted by the couple called van Loo, an extremely devoted and sympathetic Dutch couple, who were very active in the Sufi movement. They had been busy for many years with the supervision of the construction of the Dargah and in the long run came also meditation sessions for devoted guests. This required an enormous amount of patience and major persuasive power among the Indian agencies and workers. Also international Sufi seminars were held in these inspiring surroundings. The tomb of Inayat Khan was an oasis of rest, beauty and love, splendidly constructed with the white marble, the red, fragrant flower aureoles which lay around it, the texts with the three most beautiful prayers of Inayat Khan, and if I remember correctly they were the Pir, Nabi and Razul. I met many people, of all religions of India, and made many friends.

I made the first trip to India, in 1989, with Sufi friend, Jala. We were well prepared in advance by my murshida, Sharifa, because it in fact concerned a pilgrimage. We were the first Sufi from the Netherlands that would visit the Dargah individually. We wanted to experience the environment and the inspiration of the place, we wanted to honour Murshid Hazrat Inayat Khan, because that was the aim of the pilgrimage, but also we wanted to lend assistance and offer our services to help Wahid van Loo and his wife. My Sufi name was Rani, which means 'queen', and I got that name just before our departure to India. I liked the name, however. As I had expected, it happened in Delhi, that if someone on the street called my name, there was teasing from the Indian youth, something like `oooh... say...' In the course of our stay Jala and I went more and more at our own pace. She was a very sympathetic woman, but tensions arose between us. This is certainly not surprising, considering the raised energy in the Dargah. I think that there was also talk of mutual jealousy, and I regret it still that I was not wiser then. I realise now, that I was at that time only a Sufi foetus, which had not yet been beaten into shape by life, I was naive, innocent, inexperienced and hypersensitive and easily offended.

Later Jala said I had changed a lot suddenly, after Herbert, my spouse, had called me from the Netherlands on the second day after our arrival in India to gain pity, which he felt he deserved since he was lonely and did not know what he would do without me. I lost my patience with him and told him to look up friends and enjoy his freedom. Well, he took this advice literally as I later understood, and when I returned from travelling there was even a large pile of dirty laundry waiting for me to do when I returned. This shocked me just the same. Our definitive split did not take long, and after girlfriend Roseanne looked him up at Akzo, where he worked, to declare her feelings for him, according to all reports, the floodgates were opened and in August 1989 I threw him out of the house. I will always be grateful to fate for having ensured that he disappeared from my life. Because the unavoidable separation could have happened very differently, since he loved himself and money very much. I was of course very shaken by the divorce, although I thought that I was okay, because I was glad that he was gone. But obviously there was a mourning process that happens in the subconscious. We had nevertheless been together nineteen years! If I look back on those years, there was a lot of chaos in my life, with innumerable problems. This happened at my work, in the Sufi group and afterwards with `the Russians', who came into my life in 1991.

A year later, in 1990, I went for the second time to India, to the Dargah, but then on my own. I had made an arrangement with Afzal Khan, a friend from the Dargah, and he came to pick me up from the airport with his wife. That second trip, which lasted approximately a month, was superb and full of remarkable events. When I stayed with the family of Afzal, I met a politician there, who hardly spoke any English, and for this reason our conversation was rather short. He did not interest me much in this way, but at a given moment Afzal approached me and said that this gentleman had invited me to open a large quarry in the region. He said he was unable and would I like to do this for him. I said a whole-hearted `yes', of course, because to me it seemed like a nice adventure. Well, that is what it was, indeed. It took place at night. With the dignitaries from that region, near Rampur, Uttar Pradesh, we left the place of residence of Afzal under a superb starry sky late in the evening, because of the coolness, to what for me was an unknown place.

In the distance I saw a large crowd of people, of course all Indians, at a large building, I believe that I was the only westerner in the whole area. We were received officially, as was usual for highly-placed individuals, and we sat in a circle and conversed with each other, and something to use. The attention was focused very much on me, I felt somewhat taken aback and uneasy. I thought, `If I now have to act like a princess, I then leave only the questions concerning the construction of the factory, production, remunerations, the female employees, what they earn and if that is just as much as the men'. Under the rapt attention of all present I asked the questions and got exhaustive and satisfactory answers. It was very interesting. 'The women earn no less than the men', I was solemnly assured. At a given moment I thought slightly nervously: 'What would Beatrix have said and done in these circumstances? and I promptly received inspiration, so that the conversation went extremely well. It was of course very entertaining for me, because I thought, 'They think I am a very important person, but who?' After this conversation we walked, surrounded by hundreds of onlookers, employees of that factory, interested parties and press, to the spot where the ceremony would take place. A couple of vips walked beside me and we talked. I joked, my neighbour started laughing, and promptly the entire mob laughed, even though they had understood nothing of our exchange. I thought: 'so this is what it's like when Beatrix is travelling', these are therefore the rituals. The ceremony itself took place at three large, hot ovens, and after two fire priests had completed their ceremonies, I was asked to throw coals into the fire using a large scoop. I did that at all three ovens, and after that Afzal's wife did this also. All those hundreds of faces disappeared into the vague gleam of the fire and the stars, two Agni priests who carried out the rituals, the particular position which I suddenly occupied, it was all an unforgettable experience...

After the first India trip Herbert and I separated after nineteen years together. Meanwhile my son Edwin graduated from Wageningen University and had married Marga, thus I had get used to another new life. I also meanwhile became a grandmother to two beautiful children, in 1987, and 1990. With a certain guilty feeling I realise now, which I did not realise at the time, that I probably was not the stereotype granny who always devotes herself to the children. No, my life had been full and tumultuous, and this has been hanging over me for many years, certainly in the period 1989 up to 1995. I was invited in May 1992 by Murshid Haseem to visit the Sufi Circle at the Sufi camp in Canada, at Lake O'Hara, high in the Rocky Mountains. The superb, emerald-coloured lake lay at 2000 meters altitude and we were with approximately 60 Canadian 'lovers of Truth'. It was an inspiring event, there were activities of the inner school, the universal worship (with a living altar of 15 people, which was the first time this had ever been done), Sufi dance, zikr's and meetings around the campfire. I remember that something very remarkable happened there. One day, during the camp, a

Canadian girl had some problems, it seemed due to the high level of energy and the workshops and she seemed to lose her senses. I also saw that happen and suddenly she was excluded from the group activities. I did not ask someone where she was as I wasn't acquainted with her, but sympathised a lot with her. Someone told me that she was sick and would be absent for a couple of days, but that she was in good hands. Haseem and the others had taken responsibility for her destiny and supported her intensively. I frequently thought of her and hoped that she would shortly be OK again. A couple of days later she came back to the group, a bit pale but much better. I went up to her, welcomed her and said that I was very glad that she was there. She looked at me and said: `I am also glad to see you. I want to thank you warmly for the fact that you have been with me continuously during my sickness. It has helped me an awful lot'. I looked at her incredulously, because I had not been to visit her and had not done anything at all, actually. I said: `Sorry, but I have not been with you, you are mistaken.' After my response she looked nervous as if she suddenly realised she had said something strange and she turned away. I left things be and wished her well. Later I asked Murshid Haseem, how she could have thought that I was with her, whereas this was not the case. He looked at me a little mysteriously, and said: 'Yes, that's right, you were present. But you don't remember that'. He didn't want to say much about it, but he said that I am a strong woman, and that she had needed this and as a result, was busy with me a lot. She needed my strength and could profit from it. I thought this was marvellous of course and was very glad that I could mean something to her. I still did not understand very well, but assumed that she had contact perhaps with my astral or ethereal body, and that this had helped her. I still find it a miraculous event and try to recapture this phenomenon at certain moments in my life.

Later I have experienced something similar when I was in Tibet in 1998, and lay for two days gravely ill in bed because of the altitude of more than 4000 meters. That was in Zangdu, southeast of the capital Lhasa. For two nights I heard the distant chanting and the trumpet sound of the ritual meditations of the Tibetan monks. I found it marvellous to listen, while seriously ill in bed, it put me at my ease and made me feel safer so I could sleep. I was so sick that on the first day I was convinced that I would never see the Netherlands again. Because of the Tibetan singing and the prescribed drinking of seven litres of water per day I felt much better on the third day and could continue the gruelling trip in Tibet. When I appeared in a rather feeble state next morning at the breakfast table, still weak and people at the table asked me how I was feeling, I said I felt a bit better but that I wanted to visit the monastery on the other side of the road, because for two nights, from approximately nine o'clock at night to early in the morning I had heard the monotone singing of the monks. They looked at me astonished, and then I heard that there was no monastery on the other side of the road, but a garrison of Chinese soldiers. Up to a hundred kilometres radius there was no monastery, said the tour leader. We looked at each other and everyone thought that other was crazy, I thought it of the people at the table and they thought it of me. In short, I had a look and indeed there was only one barracks with soldiers. I have deeply hidden this experience in my heart and am terrible happy. Later I have heard that Tibetan monks in their monasteries long ago communicated with each other in this astral manner and could hear each other's song up to hundreds of kilometres away, and that this was part of their spiritual trainings. Obviously have I caught something from the 'akasha', perhaps did I have contact with a monastery from former times? Perhaps that girl in Canada also had such an experience with me, and that she has been helped as a result, just like I have.

Up to March 1992 I helped Haseem, the leader of the Sufi Circle, with a lot of matters such as lectures and the work concerning the booklet 'Sufi Inn', for which I had been promoted to general manager. He published that booklet personally and I was responsible for the printing and dispatch. I had a lot of work concerning this, on top of my fulltime job as administrator and other matters. Later, consistent with what the Russians already said, my integrity was undeservedly called into question by the Sufi bosses, they accused me falsely of using the Caravan address database for the Russians concerned. I'll tell more about it later. Then, in that celestial camp at Lake O'Hara, in June 1992, I had a number of conversations with the Canadian representative of the Sufi Circle, and a couple of Canadian friends; they made me see that Murshid Haseem `expected a lot of me' and that he hoped that I would entirely dedicate my life to Sufism. During this conversation we stood by the sea coast at Vancouver, I peered anxiously into the water and understood that I was being given a task, of which I doubted in large degree if I was up to it. I reacted hesitantly and in no way positively. I have frequently been in such a situation, like at the Theosophists, where someone also expected much of me, and at the Freemasons. I never understood why they liked me: `What do they want of me, do they want to recruit me for their cause? I am indeed a hard worker and also a good, conscientious worker, perhaps that is what they want. I have been spiritually focused and have my ideals, thus perhaps I am able to achieve something. But in that chaotic time that subject was not spent on me. Now there was a fly in the ointment, as a result of which such a development was no longer likely at the Sufi Circle, at least in my opinion. In March 1992 something unpleasant had happened between me and the leader concerned, and I felt that my position in the Sufi Circle, however undesirable to the concerned parties, could no longer be the same. Certainly not in the field of faith and naivety, which is what concerns me. That was in the past, but nobody knew about it.

Also I realised myself, that the Sufi Circle was not the ultimate goal for me, there was still more to come in my life, but I had no idea what. I realised, that this intuition was separate from my connection, my respect and love for Murshid Hazrat Inayat Khan. It had more to do with the hierarchical structure of the Sufi Circle, with the environment of officials in the higher echelons (an ex-minister and a couple of diplomats), and for me this meant: a type of inflexibility, detachment, arrogance, hypocrisy, conservatism, autocracy etc., but also kindness. The Arab language was used intensively for names, titles, mystic singing, indeed the complete flow chart was even in Arabic, with names which sounded like Arabic music. When in 1990, together with my Indian Sufi friend Afzal, I visited Murshida in the Banstraat, he said after he had examined several images on the wall: `Rani, this is all just Islam! Sufism is simply Islam!' I found this to be not so important, therefore I did not react. I must say, however, that the use of the exotic Arab language gave a mysterious, exotic touch and a mystic, enigmatic environment. There were enough people who were impressed by it, perhaps unconsciously, and were proud of their flowery names. Once I translated, for myself, a number of job titles and job descriptions from a flow chart into Dutch, and I had to laugh, when I saw how totally different the implications became, something like that of old Dutch: a feeling of ' take it easy, things are crazy enough as it is' ....These positions seemed to rather lose their magic. This was of course separate from the real meaning and content of the jobs, but I will not go into that. That was a serious matter and needed serious people. Characteristic of the influence of the diplomats was the hierarchical ranking and the spiritual ranks and degrees, and the polite distance that went along with it, 'personal space' (as it is called nowadays) with respect to each other. This was also the case at the inner school. There was a system of degrees of spiritual development that had been established, and at inception you were grouped into class 1, 2 or 3 etc. as the grading was stipulated by the higher echelons, and the ordinary Sufis had no say in the matter. They could only be satisfied, envious or hurt, depending on their information on the `grading' of their fellow men.

If there is one person who would reject this in my opinion, it is Pir-o-Murshid Hazrat Inayat Khan. Hypocrisy is to be found in the denial and suppression of one's own psychological shadow, to the detriment of the other. When crisis moments arise in life, where the shadowy aspects are addressed, the result is the well-known projection of one's own negativity onto others, who then get the blame. As *we* are the good ones without any trace of evil intentions...

Due to all kinds of events, I began to let go of some of my original ideas in relation to Sufism from 1990 onwards. The image of Murshid Inayat Khan faded slightly for me. I knew what inspiration and spirituality I could have received from him, and assumed that there was an astral Sufi Circle, in which he still plays a role. And I want to dedicate myself to that! On earth as well however, his death was not without consequences for the organisation that he had established. If the founder, theMessenger dies, the original, spiritual impulse tends to fade, and is at best kept alive for a while by his students. I remember for example, that a Sufi in Canada told me that Murshid, just before his last trip to India, had declared to his mureed, Shamcher Beorse, that he would eradicate the hierarchical structure, which he had installed in the Sufi Circle, on his return from India. He saw that this system did not work favourably for his organisation and the disharmony among his students was reinforced by jealousy and conflicts.

In 1997, I wrote an article, entitled `Contemplation: what is the Sufism of Hazrat Inayat Khan in 1997, and beyond?' There was a willingness to publish the article in the booklet Sufia, of the Sufi community, although at that time I had already distanced myself from the Sufi organisations. I cite from the Article:

`A frequently returning subject in my ideas is: how the Sufism of Murshid Hazrat Inayat Khan would be viewed if he were here now and his message would now be spread? Then one should reflect as follows: Inayat Khan appeared in another time - at the beginning of the twentieth century - in the west and developed the form of his message in that period. He died in 1927. His message of love, harmony and beauty inspired many. He claimed that there is a divine being, a being which exists in us and works through us: the spirit of guidance, which was involved in the founding of religions and cultures, and as a result turned the universal brotherhood of man into a fact. The beginning of the twentieth century was a different time to now. I can imagine that he was involved with people that, more than now, lived in a world of more concrete space for example, there were the workers who had to fight for their living and the more privileged classes existed, there was a clear class distinction, in his own country he had to deal with English dominance, in the west with the rise of industry and especially in America with the start of a new world. Much was invented in that time and afterwards, which for us are now well-known products. In Europe he came in contact with all kinds of people. Because of his refined spirit and culture he met people who were artists and nobility and other related spirits. It was clear that this was the result of his refined being and individuality, enabling his message to be passed on. After his death his message was further spread by his children and family who succeeded in keeping the essence and nature, the flame of his message, burning brightly. And then I think to myself: how would Inayat Khan act now?

After his death so much has happened on this planet: a world war, developments in technology, growing antagonisms between cultures which are used to commit dreadful crimes, in the west society has been engulfed by consumerism, production and material prosperity. There were large shifts of ethnic groups, the west was and is still faced with mass immigration of people from Africa, Asia, and Eastern Europe wishing to make an economic improvement in their life. Because of this the meeting of several cultures and religions in the west has progressed considerably, and there are now only very few who have not already become familiar, also in their immediate surroundings, with several exotic cultures and religions. There are many problems of an economic nature, of a cultural nature and of a human nature which have arisen... The time has now come for us to learn how to approach diversity: outside ourselves, but at the same time inside ourselves! Differences such as antagonisms, confrontations between old and new, perhaps eventually, with 'our old selves and our new selves'...? How would Inayat Khan define this 'new self'? His message must have provided the first impetus for this nevertheless! The new self clearly has a planetary intention, a growth towards wholeness, a universality of our thinking and being. Looking outside of and growing beyond our small circle. This demands considerable effort, a separate concerted effort of every person. The will to grow, the quantum leap ... For this reason I think that Inayat Khan in the first place would have explained the term 'brotherhood' further. Brotherhood ties in with the development of the frequently regretted concept of individuality in present times, which has exceeded its aim and brought only loneliness and misery. Developing the term 'brotherhood' means: who am I, how do I relate to others, how can I find my 'wholeness' as a person and my relationship with God and the world? What do we have to do to achieve this?

The vehicle of the new message of Inayat Khan would have to be a 'workplace'. How? We would first have to ask the following questions: how do we handle authority? How does authority or hierarchy treat us? Do we have to surround ourselves with the sociability and security of an organisation with its hierarchy, or do we take the opportunity in this life to establish our place in the cosmos and acquire an identity, however and wherever? Can we muster up the courage for this? Do we have the pain left for that? I think that Inayat Khan would consider it of great importance in the current era that people really discover their own being, and he would agree with C. Verschaeve:

> *To be someone is to have one's own being,*
> *With one's own being traits: nature,*

language, name, destiny; to feel one's own stream of life and to have therein yet another life, a world within a world, to be a wholeness and to take one's place in the fullest sense in the harmony of everything.

Would this be the 'model' for the future person that Inayat Khan had in mind?

The Sufi Circle later split up, halfway through the 20th century, and moreover the Sufi Commune was instigated, overseen by the eldest son of Inayat Khan, Pir Waseem Khan. A couple of smaller Sufi branches also sprung up.

The Universal Worship
I was initiated on 12 June 1986 into the Sufism of the Sufi Circle, and up to the summer of 1989 there were a couple of fairly quiet years, in which I followed the Sufi classes and hoped to be initiated as cheraga (light-bearer) eventually and to take part in the Universal Worship created by Inayat Khan. This was a splendid ceremony: an altar with the sacred books of the six major religions: Hinduism, Buddhism, Zoroastrianism, Islam, Judaism, Christianity and six candelabras and candles. There was a seventh candle which was 'dedicated to all those who, knowingly or unknowingly, have upheld the light of truth'.

During the universal worship two cherags stand at the altar, one of them lights the candles, whereupon a short text is read from the holy book of the concerned religion, and after a text concerning the same subject has also been cited from the remaining holy books, the second cherag holds a short sermon, based on this text. We wore long, black mantles or habits, which were later replaced by dark brown mantles. If we followed the universal worship with our spiritual eye from the small room, we were able to observe sometimes that, during the worship, an illuminated shape would appear above and around the altar and the cherags, and later after the sermon this light, or energy, poured out over the congregation during the pronouncement of an invocation. Later, in the Russian orthodox church, it seemed to me that during the liturgical worship, the divine liturgy, by the priest, such a broad `airlock' for the light was created above, an 'airlock' as it were to the divine world, to God. At the end of the service this light and this blessing is poured out by the priest to the churchgoers. It seems to me, that this light is always created anew during the liturgy and on one day it is possibly more intensive and more noticeable than on another.

The spiritual experiences, as I have described them so far, have had a serious influence on my life. I have always been glad about what I had been taught and/or have observed, because I was intuitively gifted, but I could not place those experiences, I could not incorporate them into my own life. I had the idea that I remained as I was, had thereby little faith in other people, and had unconsciously even, to my shame, little faith in my Sufi teacher, Murshida. Perhaps it was significant that she had been the director of my high school, of whom we were all rather frightened. I played the `game' of the other Sufi's and tried to make myself useful. I could not however rid myself of the idea that: `it can't be true, all this beauty cannot really be intended for me' and then I think of that little girl in the Japanese camp, who had the same thoughts upon hearing that her father was gone forever. I think that I wrestled with a double handicap: the little girl in the Japanese camp, but also a type of intuition I experienced that there had to be more, I was not easily satisfied. It seemed all too easy, as if to say `is that all there is?

I had not yet become aware that the splendid insight that I sought was already inside me. I looked too much to the external world and expected to receive enlightenment by means of the outside world, by means of masters etc. I had not yet understood that God is recognisable in our inner self, as well as Christ and the saints of this world and that we must focus our attention inwards. That is not easy and there is even courage necessary, because our processes of change take place by means of that inner self! By means of intention and strength of will, dedication, vision, humility, love and courage. It concerns the principle 'know Thyself'! Murshid Hazrat Inayat Khan taught me:

> 'What do we reach by meditation? Do we want power, do we do want inspiration? No, above all we wish most for an image of our true self; that is, to stand face to face with our innermost self. Then we experience the presence of God, we no longer need to search for the rewards of Heaven, because we are in search of God in ourselves. For this reason it is necessary that every initiated individual knows that the aim of our soul in our esoteric study and exercises is to make ourselves familiar with life as a moving flow in the circle of perpetuity.'
> Nasihat.

If I think back to that, the marvellous teachings of Inayat Khan which I received in the classes and during the universal celebrations, my visits to the Dargah, his tomb in New Delhi, my visit to the Tilak house at the Jamoena river, where he had lived and died, made an unforgettable, loving impression on me. I have even been able to meditate for a while in his chamber in the Tilak house, which made a big impression on me. I had very pleasant contact with his family members, who now played an important role in Sufism and whom I appreciated very much. This all left me still with 'no clue'. I considered the spiritual experiences more as a great adventure of the psyche, which I did not have to take seriously. I found that one frequently 'borrows rank', something to improve one's own image. There was always an air of mystery around the 'vips', as I called the higher initiated ladies and gentlemen, and most are breathless when having to address these extremely important individuals.

There were ex-diplomats or ambassadors and/or their spouses and famous artists. But I was not very impressed by this environment.

* * *

Chapter 6. 1989: Meeting with three spiritual Russians

Destiny obviously dictated that, at a given moment, I needed some rest in my rather busy life and I promptly had an accident a week before my birthday, in 1991. I stumbled on the street and shattered my left ankle. I stayed a couple of weeks in the Red Cross hospital, got a number of screws and plates in my ankle and was incapacitated for eight months.

Miraculously, a few days before this accident, during a walk in the dunes, I met two girlfriends whom I had not seen for at least twenty years. They were the ones who helped me through the eight months, taking care of me when I could not walk. Through our conversations one of them was seized by the message of Inayat Khan, and she explored this topic further. She was a reporter at an important newspaper and told me later that these teachings had helped her and at a given moment she even got a good position on the editorial team of her newspaper. She worked there very successfully and worked in the spirit of Hazrat Inayat Khan, as she said herself. Then a couple of years later in the Sufi temple in Katwijk when she interviewed the leader Haseem, whom I knew well, she mentioned my name and told him that she was a friend of mine and that she had come to Sufism thanks to me. The leader concerned blinked his eyes, according to her story and asked someone beside him: `Do I know that person?', to which that person concerned replied `yes'. As the world turns... perhaps he would have known if my Sufi name had been mentioned: Maharani?

Why did the spiritual leader concerned blink his eyes? A special tale begins.

During the annual international Sufi summer school in the Sufi temple in Katwijk, which was held in August, lasted a month and was visited by Sufi from all over the world, from South Africa to Canada, from Sweden to Italy, I had several tasks. Outside of my governing board activities, I also sometimes sat at the entrance of the Sufi temple doing various administrative odd jobs, such as selling tickets and programmes, and providing information.

In that year, 1991, in the Sufi Circle, it was whispered that Russians would come to the summer school. That was of course extremely interesting, because who would have the opportunity to meet Russians at that time? The wall had just fallen, but Yeltsin had not yet come to power in Russia. There was therefore no free movement of persons still and few had ever met Russians. One day in August 1991 I sat at the entrance of the Sufi temple to verify the registrations and reservations. Someone whispered to me: `There are the Russians!' I was surprised and saw an interesting person standing in front of my table, a nice-looking fifty-something, who could have stepped out of a Russian icon of Christ. He was with a friend. I took the opportunity, stood up and introduced myself to them. He introduced himself as Vsevolod from Moscow, and his friend was called Kliment. To my surprise I felt a little nervous. We had a conversation and I asked him if he could me tell something concerning their life in Russia. He started talking and I was very captivated by his tale, concerning travelling in Russia with his friends, concerning visits to dervishes and shamans, to convents and communities in Siberia, concerning contacts with mystics all over Russia. I thought at a given moment: `What a beautiful, romantic tale. It is typical, but this man is telling me about exactly the things in which I have a special interest such as profound, romantic and adventurous books, such as those of Paul Brunton': `He is deceiving me, he tells me what I want to hear and he knows exactly what that is, because he reads it in my astral body...' I laughed at myself, and found this incident funny, even if his tale was not entirely in line with reality. Then he entered the hall and we said a cordial farewell. That year I had contact with Vsevolod a couple of times, I brought them in my car to people they wanted to meet, but the year after, in 1992, when they came to the Sufi summer school, the contact would become more intensive.

The Sufi's received the Russians, and in 1991 that was Vsevolod and Kliment, a forty-something and Cossack from Moscow, and their friends, among whom an artist, Tamara, who made beautiful portraits of a number of Sufi vips, very cordially. During their stay in the summer school, which lasted a month, they visited somewhere almost every evening. Everyone was elated and there was something of a buzz of excitement, hope and expectation, perhaps Vsevolod would play an important role in the Sufi Circle! I could not attend what I heard was an impressive lecture which Vsevolod held at the end of that summer school, to my regret. But I had some deep conversations with him, when I took them in my car a couple of times to their next appointment. At that time, in 1991, as far as I knew, hardly anyone knew that Vsevolod and Kliment themselves had come with a spiritual message to the west.

But now back to August 1992, therefore the following year. There was a summer school again and during a break I sat outside with a couple of people and saw that Vsevolod was there. I was glad to see him, because I had now and then thought of him with the idea that there was something special about him and it would be nice to meet him and talk to him again. Then, here he was. I stood up from the table and walked up to Vsevolod, welcomed him and said that I was glad to see him again. He reacted in a somewhat more distant manner than the previous year, but pleasantly. I was a little surprised about that, but could find absolutely no reason for it. We talked a little and went our separate ways. Later a man in his thirties appeared and in unintelligible English tried to tell me something concerning the Russian Sufism. This proved to be one of the workers of Vsevolod, who had come with him from Russia to the summer school. He was called Georgy and was half Georgian and half Russian. I listened to him without having the slightest idea about what he was talking about, but I thought: 'what beautiful eyes!' This time a large group of Russian mystics had come, who were interested in Western Sufism. Kliment was not there and Georgy looked a bit like him, but looked more friendly. I immediately had the feeling that I knew him well as if he was an old friend of mine. I had, in fact, from the first meeting with Vsevolod and Kliment, the feeling that I knew them a long time, but with Georgy this feeling was strongest and most clear. I invited them to dine with me. Vsevolod said that in the Russian group there was a dancer who practised Indian dancing and that she wanted to show her art to me. In short, that evening the companionship would be my guest and I picked them up. With me in the car were Vsevolod, Georgy and Parvaiz, Sufi from Novosibirsk, a city somewhere deeply in Siberia. We sat in the car waiting until the whole group was in the car and then we chatted. Then Parvaiz, who in the back of the car, took something from his pocket and handed over it to me, saying that this photograph was important for me. I looked at to the photograph and gasped in amazement. It was a rare photograph, an image of the master Morya, whom I knew from Theosophy. It was almost thirty years ago, that the then Theosophical leader, Mr Kork, gave me two rare images of the masters Morya and Koot Hoomi, who at the end of the nineteenth, or beginning of the twentieth century commissioned Helena Petrovna Blavatsky to spread theosophical knowledge throughout the world. It was said that these masters lived, and still live, somewhere in the Himalayas, in Shambalah. I still remember that I was very impressed then, especially as one of the two photographs was very like someone whom I dreamt of in Italy. And one of these photographs, that of Master Morya, I now held in my hand and that had come to me all the way from Siberia ...! Was this by chance, a sign? I did not know what to think of it, but I knew that chance does not exist. I considered it as a renewed contact with distant times... That evening was interesting: Georgy offered to help in the kitchen and proved to be a good cook. The Indian dancing was well carried out and I got to hear many tales concerning Russia. In that time I frequently had pain in my back and neck and Vsevolod, who saw I had problems, said that Georgy could help me, because Georgy was an excellent faith healer. Georgy massaged some points in my neck and shoulders, sometimes pressing firmly, and within ten minutes I was feeling better. I again had the feeling that I already knew him for a long time.

The Russians and I met each other therefore during the summer school in 1992, and we met a number of times to come to my home with a group of Dutch and Russian Sufi. That became a lively affair. There was a kind of recognition from the beginning. I was very fond of them and called Vsevolod, Georgy and Kliment `my three brothers, who have returned from the Universe'. I found other Russian Sufis less interesting. I had, of course, the Russian vodka initiation, which was not entirely new to me, and we talked, danced and amused ourselves.

I remember how Vsevolod once initiated me, when we were on the pier at the lighthouse in Scheveningen, in the style of the novel concerning Don Quichot, into the knighthood of the order of Saint

Bonaventura and Saint Jurgen, 'they', he said, 'know how to work with space and time properly.' I also remember that we sat for a time under the large beech trees by the pond in Clingendael. Vsevolod drew a triangle on the ground with a branch with a heart in the middle. 'The angles,' he remarked, 'represent our strange triad: Georgy, Kliment and I, and the heart in the middle is you.' I later had a small, golden brooch of this symbol made.

I remember that, if I walked on the street beside Vsevolod, I frequently had the strange sensation that I was floating, I felt myself become very light, also in my head. I found it unpleasant, but saw it as nervousness and thought no further. In the Sufi summer school everyone was very cordial to them, and did their best to make living in the Netherlands agreeable for them. That year, in September 1992, I succeeded, together with a vip from the Sufi Circle, in extending the tourist visa of Vsevolod and Georgy by a month, so they could remain in the Netherlands, to look around and expand their contacts. Of those contacts they kept up a system, they wrote the name of everyone with whom they had spoken, with their address and phone number. And they were to come and stay with me.

Now I got to know the nice and less nice sides of the company. The nice ones included for example the moment that I went for the first time with Vsevolod and Georgy to the hypermarket. We would do grocery shopping together and they would cook at night. We were hardly in the hypermarket when I felt that my arms were being clasped left and right. They held on to me and looked around astonished. They were impressed by the abundance of products. They were not used to something like this in Russia. Thus they remained standing and looking in astonishment at the luxurious cans of cat and dog food, their eyes wide.

I remember from my visit to Russia in March 1993, that the shops were small and inconspicuous, like private houses. You could buy things there, in somewhat dim light and after that stand in line while a young lady charged up the products by means of an old-fashioned cash register at a pay-desk. Sometimes with handwritten receipt, which you had to then deliver somewhere. Well, during grocery shopping in the supermarket in The Hague we held on to each other and that pleased me very much! I found it very sociable. When we passed by a terrace afterwards, a lady who was drinking coffee with friends called out: `Hey, that's unfair! I have only one at home! I gave a wink her and continued further, feeling satisfied. They stayed with me and I went every day to my work. I was administrator at a youth care agency and had do a lot of work there, because we were in the middle of a merger. Therefore that meant much extra work. Well, then I became aware, I think, of the cultural difference. On the second day we had an appointment in the morning that they would do the grocery shopping and cook in the evening, then I didn't need to do that. I went happily to my work. When I came home at six o'clock at night the house was empty, the windows were wide open, it had rained and there was no sign of my guests, there had been a storm, however, and only a mess was left behind. No note or other sign, and in the days afterwards even no phone call. Nothing. They stayed away for a week. Suddenly they reappeared Saturday morning in front of me. I was glad to see them, because I had been frustrated. I did not have any idea how to react to the situation. When I said something, they answered: 'Oh, we visited some people and then we just stayed'. Naturally I said I could understand, but that they could have informed me. They did this to me once or twice more afterwards. I was too disconcerted to adequately react. How should I interpret this? Later I understood that it was not cultural difference, but perfectly ordinary insolence. I had not completely got used to something like this, had never experienced it before and so I just stood there in astonishment. Now that no longer happened, but I had been numbed by this blunt manner. I considered them as my friends, as my guests, and I had been considered very welcoming and not at all awkward. Also I had not got used to the fact, that my whisky and wine stock was entirely plundered in an extremely short time, and if I replaced it, conscientiously, the same happened again. I therefore stopped replacing it. Also at the Sufi my Russian friends ensured surprises. I remember that Vsevolod stayed during the Sufi summer school in 1992, with a friendly Sufi diplomat's family in Wassenaar. One evening at my home, he indicated that he would also like to stay with me. Georgy had already moved in to my place a couple of days before. Well, that was fine with me. He wanted to move in straight away and pick up his luggage. It was around midnight, therefore I said that it was impossible, because his host and hostess were perhaps already in bed. No, that was not the case, he knew that those people would have no objection. 'Obliging as always' and without thinking further, drove I them to Wassenaar just after midnight. Vsevolod had the key, went in to the house to get his luggage and I waited with Georgy. Because of the late hour, I was rather uneasy about it. After fifteen minutes or so Vsevolod came outside with his overnight bag. He told me that he had been very quiet, but that his host suddenly appeared in his pyjamas. He was astonished and asked what was going on? He explained this to him and then left with the overnight bag. Later I was denounced for this by this family, and others, but that was understandable. I should have been wiser and more cautious, and told Vsevolod that he could also move in the next day, however. But then I had little time, because I had to go to work, that was the problem.

They visited parties in their honour at the Sufi, especially where ladies were present, and that was what it was all about, according to the tales, because I myself was never there, but they apparently consumed a lot of strong alcohol and such. The women were delighted with these handsome Russians, and the Russians, supposedly as well as the women, did not seem to know what had hit them with all this attention and flirting. Supposedly they taught the ladies by means of the `teaching situations ' of their School, as they did in Russia, and that was initially seen as interesting. But the expectations which they had awoken were later unfulfilled and some ladies were very dissatisfied in the end. I heard that you should not be surprised if you entered such a private house only to be suddenly confronted by a Sufi lady (with class) totally naked and waving a knife and crying: `Come on! Where is God!' Later it became clear to me, that the gentlemen in Russia also did not treat their womenfolk in a gentle manner.

The vips in the Sufi Circle appeared to think that I had organised those `lewd' incidents! At the end of 1992, for example, a Sufi lady had been so kind as to offer her empty house to the Russians, so that they could hold their meetings there. And, to my amazement, another vip lady then told me sadly that she had put the mattresses there before the parties...! And I was therefore also guilty, because I helped the Russians to organise all of that!!! I did not know exactly what she was referring to, but it presumably concerned alcohol and sex. Although I had not frequently been present at the activities in that house and never experienced anything lewd, I thought of putting her mind at rest by saying everything would be fine, however. But that did not help.

These Russians did not know how to behave themselves in relation to women, or rather, ladies. They had obviously never heard of rules of decency and respect, and that a woman is something different to a man, and is not a disposable commodity. How they treated Russian women, I heard later, was also not very decent. I understood later that it concerned strong women, tough and hateful towards men and that, especially in the Moscow mystic underground circles, this indicated the tone of the company there. The Soviet government had always been favourable towards women and according to the tales a lot of men in Russia had been the victim of this, being convinced to marry, allowing the woman to move in to the man's flat, divorce papers being served and the man being ultimately thrown out of the flat. This was legally possible. Our three Russians were extremely macho and later it became clear to me, that a woman, and certainly her feelings, did not count in their eyes. The word 'respect' was not known to them. Later a female Sufi, a collaborator of Pir Vaseem Khan, told me that the Russians were not at all in touch with their inner female side and that I should not worry about their behaviour. Furthermore I observed in the gentlemen that 'the end justifies the means' was considered as their work model. What was extremely painful was the way they treated one of those ladies, however. She had expectations after the Russians had stayed with her and appeared to like Georgy especially, as she told me in confidence. Anticipating their return to the Netherlands (because they were in Russia) she began taking Russian lessons. She was a nice, spiritual, Dutch woman.

They quickly dropped her like a hot potato and I remember still, with pain in my heart, how she sat in the house on the van der Aastraat, the house in question, where the Russians had stayed in December 1992, and held their workshops, as a broken woman beside Vsevolod. I heard her say: 'but I thought that you were my friends!' Vsevolod sat calmly beside her. I thought he was like 'the fox in the bushes', a thought that has crossed my mind several times since ...

I do not know what they did to her, what had happened. It still causes me pain if I think about it, though I had nothing to do with it and did not know what expectations had been awoken. I didn't know what I had to do, should I interfere and ask questions about what is going on? When I asked Georgy about that, the answer was naturally that there was nothing wrong. Later the same woman said to me: 'Oh, you are with Georgy, well okay then, that's fine'. I was a bit astonished. It seemed as if she was distancing herself, but from what? No, that was not nice at all. I appeared to be in a corner, which I couldn't get out of, because I was very keen on Georgy, with all his charm.

It was the most normal thing in the world for my three friends that the woman paid everything, mostly me therefore, and that by means of the moral and financial support of this woman for their School, they had had marvellous opportunities in the Netherlands, and indeed in the west. This best friend, who always helped them, me in other words, would also prove to be a disposable item eventually. But that will come later. When I met Georgy in August 1992 in Katwijk, something immediately happened within me. He was a lot younger than me, more than twenty years, and although I wanted to have him as a friend, I did not think of a serious relationship and certainly not marriage. I had just separated, in 1990, and was very satisfied with my free, creative life. I did a lot with friends and acquaintances, went out in my blue Saab, met interesting people, such as the Ajib Brothers, world famous Indian traditional music group, who gave concerts at my home. They invited me as their most important guest for their concert in London and also to come to Lahore, where they lived. A friend of theirs, Azat, told me that I would experience in Lahore some special things: the Brothers were very popular there and were so revered that people threw themselves on the ground if they passed by, and according to him, that would happen also to me...

I went to Canada, the Rocky Mountains, to a Sufi camp, I did governing board work for the Sufi order, as a result of which I had contact with people all over the world. Sometimes I was called from Australia, then from Canada, and this went on like that. I organised house concerts with students of the Royal Academy, where my piano teacher gave lessons, and they did this gladly as an exercise for their final examination. We made music with open windows and the next day, to my relief, I got positive responses from the neighbours, such as `such beautiful music was played' and that they `had enjoyed it'. I still could have been more active in the Sufi Order, but here I encountered some issue, because I got into conflicts with the vips and things did not always go my way. Later I discovered that, without my knowledge, I became embroiled in the middle of plots between two vip ladies.

I will tell you something more about this:
It concerned my initiation to cheraga, which is an official position of the universal worship of Inayat Khan, and I gladly wanted to do this. A number of months before this it had been promised to me, that I would be initiated during the summer school, in August. A date was determined and I had to prepare myself. My murshida Sharifa, who would initiate me, had broken her foot at that time and lay in the hospital. It was arranged that Wahida van Loo, Sufi murshida would initiate me. I was pleased about this, because I valued her very much. I appeared that day at the agreed time, in the afternoon at approximately half past one, in the room of the Sufi temple, where a universal worship service would be organised. This was considered a good occasion for the students present, as learning material, to become familiar with this initiation ceremony.

Before I left the house I had read the text of this initiation, together with my mother, who moreover never wanted to know anything of my Sufi activities, and for the first time she had been very positive and found the text splendid. I also thought this and I was under the impression that I could experience this. I arrived respectfully and humbly at the agreed time in the room, which was full of students. The officials and witnesses at this initiation were present and wore their black robes. I went and sat happily and full of expectation on a chair in the room. I would be called. Twenty minutes before the universal worship would start I was called upon to report to Raidah, one of the vips. She invited me to meet and we entered an office beside the room. She sat opposite me. What followed was totally unexpected: after a confused introduction I got to hear that the initiation would not take place. I did not know what happened to me and, numb with fear, I thought: `I have done something terrible...' she addressed me admonishingly, and due to the shock I caught only half of what she said. I do not remember her words any longer exactly, but what I understood of it I found utterly crazy. I found that she was mixed up in matters that did not concern her. My astonishment was complete on hearing her finish by saying: `that I should first ensure my relationship with Murshida Sharifa was in order'. I was not aware that this would be necessary; I always thought I had good contact with her. Perhaps my relationship with her, as my murshida, was not exactly what it should be, because of the fact that she was the director of my high school and everyone (including me) was rather frightened of her. Perhaps I had not yet put this behind me.

Totally confused and upset I made my way out of the room via the back door. There Azim, fellow mureed, stood looking at me pityingly and even whispered: `what have they done now'. I drove home. It was a bleak, foggy day. My mother, who lived at home downstairs, came to me. She looked at me expectantly, and said then, knowingly: `it didn't go ahead, then'. and then, before I could have said something, she said: `they had to dismiss that Kader-aga. He is not good at his work'. (Kader-aga was the big boss of the whole operation). She always supported me and stood by me. Much later I heard a consultation with a number of vips at the universal worship concerning a cryptic note which had been written by Murshida from the hospital and that concerned my initiation. Cryptic, because she had indicated in a vague manner that there was something not quite in order with my initiation. Later I understood that it concerned who would initiate me, and that Murshida had indicated that she found that she should do it. The vips obviously did not want any problems with her, since she had a bone to pick with them and perhaps felt she was offended... They chose therefore to send home the candidates fifteen minutes before the start of what was, for every mureed (student), an important initiation.

Many Sufi spoke afterwards about the disgrace of the way this had happened. It had become an issue, because I did not accept it, and found that the way it was done testified to a lack of human respect. Murshida van Loo got in contact with me the same afternoon because she did not want me to be `hurt by these careless words'. I was touched by this sympathy for a mureed, caught in the crossfire between two Sufi vip ladies. I subsequently resigned with immediate effect from my job as secretary of the governing board of Sufi and I did not appear at the temple there for some time. But now, due to my meeting with the Russians, I had entered an exciting phase, and that pleased me. I had already told Murshida Sharifa that I had : `the feeling with the Russians that I have moved from a suffocating dark back room to the top of a mountain, with a full view and tingling, fresh air'. I was not yet aware then of how stressful it would become, and how many scratches and wounds I would thereby incur. Anyhow, by the end of 1992 Georgy had moved in with me and in June 1993 we married.

It became clear fairly fast that Vsevolod wished to create a spiritual atmosphere in which his message could be received. At the beginning of February 1993 we set up the 'School Foundation' with Vsevolod and some other people, established at my address in The Hague. I was founder and treasurer; Vsevolod was chairman and Georgy secretary. I assured them that they could 'consider my house their own' because as always I was idealistic and full of good will... Although I was more focused on Sufism, I thought that Vsevolod had a lot to tell. I saw that he was informed about Theosophy and according to him they had also contacts with the Nakshibandi order in Southern Russia. Those were Muslim Sufi and the Sufi Circle of Inayat Khan was, as becomes clear from the candles on the altar of its universal worship, aimed at the six world religions, and the seventh candle had been dedicated to 'those, who knowingly or unknowingly revered the light of Truth'. What I then discovered was that Vsevolod was considered by a number of Russians to be a hermetic master. Those Russian mureeds were at the summer school in Katwijk, because the Sufi had already met Wahid and Wahida van Loo in Moscow and would have been initiated by them. The Sufi Circle had financed their trip to the Netherlands. Vsevolod thought it would be good if his followers went to the Sufi movement and had even sent them there 'for their development', as he said. The word 'hermetic' meant very little to the Western Sufi and it took a long time before I myself had a reasonable picture of Russian Hermeticism.

Vsevolod was not striving, as he told me, to have a pack of followers, because his School had not been organised formally, like the Sufi Circle, but functioned informally. Apart from the fact that he had a personal, spiritual message, there was no structure, no organisation of the 'School'. The activities of the three Russians in Russia, at the fall of the Soviet regime, had been diverse and their spiritual orientation had been directed more towards paganism, as I understood. In fact, in my opinion, they themselves were also still searching, Kliment and Georgy most certainly, Vsevolod probably also, because in my opinion he had not yet been 'that' when we met him in the Netherlands. He had a high opinion of himself and his mission. So far they had held seminars concerning spiritual development in the Baltic States and in Moscow and Saint Petersburg, and Vsevolod's followers were fairly firmly joined to him.

Later I found out that the phenomenon of a spiritual master was quite common in Russia and that such a master often collects an alternating group of followers around them who spend a shorter or longer period of time with the master, that this dynamic event was not comparable to the image and the manner of working and presentation of the Sufi Circle, and then we have not yet even mentioned the vodka... Such a group functioned underground, because in the time of the Soviet Union it had been prohibited to occupy itself with esoteric and/or religious matters. Furthermore such groups moved rapidly to remain inconspicuous and never stayed too long in one spot. Living in Russia was hard, very hard and my three Russian friends appeared thus full of fears and traumas, especially if the word 'police' was used. They characterised themselves, especially in the beginning, by means of a charming, but rather ponderous manner of action, rather 'barbaric' as I still call it, and by their nonchalance they caused a lot of damage, not only in the Sufi Circle but also where they were visiting as guests.

Much later I understood that they were in a certain way programmed products of the phenomenon of the Moscow mystic underground circles, of which they had many years experience, and while they called themselves spiritual, there was no true human civilisation and mutual consideration to be found there. There was much drinking there, partying, bullying, offensive behaviour, people were burned, kicked into the gutter, in short: there was not much more than an attempt to survive or to try to exist and make things count. This is what I was told and this can be read in Kliment's books concerning the Russian mystic underground movements. But Vsevolod continued to hope that he would find people there who would accept his teachings and follow him. He wanted to find a small, select group that would understand and spread his hermetic message. And now he was in the Netherlands.

The first year in the Netherlands they did not escape the culture shock, but unfortunately no-one recognised that as such, least of all they themselves. They were too arrogant for that, because, as real Russians, they considered it their mission to 'convert' the spiritually backward, declining and materialistic West. This is a typically Russian tendency: the mission to the west. The first years they therefore caused a lot of pain around them, due to their incomprehension and lack of familiarity with Western culture, the result being that the vips and a number of members of the Sufi Circle turned against them.

They had now started to project their own shadow on the Russians, and: on me! I was accused of betrayal, because due to my romance with Georgy, I was rather intensively involved with the Russians. I tried many times to address the charges of the Sufi and disprove them because they were undeserved and this could be proven. But for many years afterwards a number of them found it necessary to continue to admonish me based on these fantasy charges. It is still a riddle to me how it could have gone this far. It had supposedly to do with `power' and the Sufi VIPs noticed that Vsevolod was not just anyone and were obviously frightened of losing the power in their organisation. Initially they had certain positions in the Sufi Circle in mind for him, such as general representative of the Sufi Circle in Russia. But Vsevolod did not find that interesting, which is understandable seen from his position and his mission and he let that be known.

I supported the founding of Vsevolod's School in the Netherlands and did not suspect that the Sufi Circle would be so negative about it. I saw absolutely no coherence of our foundation with the Sufi

Circle, outside of the desired cooperation, and I certainly saw no reason for objections from their side.

Later it would appear that the message of Vsevolod to the west was hardly related to the message of Sufi Hazrat Inayat Khan. Inayat Khan preached the unity of all religions on the basis of mystic Islam, and the ethical 'love, harmony and beauty', refinement and transparency of the soul.

Vsevolod's message coincided with orthodox Christianity, hermeticism and alchemy. This would be crystallised in the course of the next few years and provides perhaps an explanation for the problems that arose with the Sufi Circle. Vsevolod was certainly not prepared to put himself out for the Sufi, because he had his own programme and aims. Personal promotion and behaviour on both sides was not always very elegant. It seemed at a certain moment that the Sufi Circle saw him as a dangerous threat, and that, in my opinion, had absolutely no grounds but originated from fears and projections of their own negativity, such as fear of the loss of control over their organisation. Vsevolod, with his most important student and assistant Kliment, and Kliment's disciple Georgy, brought much knowledge of spiritual traditions and cultures, which have existed down through the centuries, so that I myself thought in the first years that he was referring to Theosophy. Georgy tried to translate the lectures for the Dutch group into English; in the beginning this did not go well, but he gradually improved. A couple of years later he even translated the lectures into Dutch!

All this resulted in a lot of events, such as the seminar in Latvia that Georgy and I organised in May 1993, and that was unforgettable for many people, including me. This seminar had also been intended for the participation of the Sufi and Vsevolod had made arrangements with a couple of VIPs of the Sufi group in advance. Then suddenly murshid Haseem put an end to this cooperation for unclear reasons, right before the seminar. This was a shock, but we decided nevertheless to let the seminar continue. It did not make relations with the Sufi Circle any better, naturally, because Haseem Khan started to warn the Sufi about Vsevolod. Supposedly Russian mureeds (initially students of Vsevolod) had made unfavourable remarks about Vsevolod with the aim of currying favour with the Sufi Circle, because there were attractive Sufi positions in Russia to be redistributed, including that of national representative, which was initially intended for Vsevolod!

I had another major conflict with the then leader of the Sufi Circle about the foundation we had just set up. We had sent a circular about this to people, whose names and addresses were in the pocket notebooks of the Russians. I still have those notebooks. The leader Haseem Khan, and with him his followers, accused me of secretly using the names and addresses of the Sufi Inn subscribers, which were accessible to me because of my job. I had thus violated their trust, according to them, and I was untrustworthy! Well, their charge was unfounded, because we had used the address books of the Russians, and I clearly said that, but the defamation campaign continued. My reputation obviously had to be broken.

I was called, as 'suspect' mureed (student), to answer to Haseem concerning the fact that I had not first discussed the establishment of the School foundation with him and asked for his authorisation. I listened in astonishment to his elucidation and replied that I did not understand him. 'Must I then ask all esoteric organisations in The Hague and surroundings for authorisation firstly? I am nevertheless free to set up a foundation? I said. I understood nothing of his agitation, but they were all terribly angry with me. It seemed they were in a panic and (in my opinion unnecessarily) frightened that the Russians (and perhaps even I!) would hijack the Sufi Circle! The charges and the gossip concerning me have lasted many years. In the middle of 1995 I decided to conclude my membership of the Sufi Circle. The contact with my teacher, murshida Sharifa, had already decreased. She had meanwhile moved to a chique senior citizens home and I was much too busy. My departure from the Sufi Circle had, of course, nothing to do with my relationship/contact with murshid Hazrat Inayat Khan, but only with the people concerned with his message.

A new situation arose for the Russians and also for me in their relationship with the Sufi Circle in 1993. I promptly had my first violent brawl with Kliment, because he had demanded that our folder of the seminar in Latvia should be put in the envelopes of the next posting of the Sufi Inn booklet of the Sufi Circle. I was responsible, as manager of this booklet, for the posting. Because I belonged with the Russians, and the Sufi Circle were nevertheless now the enemy... I said that I could not and would not do so, because it had not been discussed with the editors of Sufi Inn and I did not wish to abuse their good faith. Then he said ' Imagine if I did it anyway'. I refused this naturally, because I was not worried. Then he nagged about the fact that I had a detrimental influence on the 'oh so important' activities of their School and that they could do without this. I remained steadfast and after that my relationship with Kliment, for this reason, was bad for many years. There was more. He was, for example, terribly jealous of the link which Georgy and I had, because he considered Georgy not only as his disciple, but also as his servant. What I saw was that Georgy was treated as a servant and had run around like crazy for both gentlemen. I was not the only one who noticed, because a number of Sufi at that time also felt that Georgy was treated badly. Georgy himself found it an honour, because, he said, in Russia this means that you are experiencing a learning process with the master.

I was therefore very 'lucky' with my three Russian friends. Unfortunately I have since that time been unable to take their spiritual message very seriously, no matter how interesting the lectures were; I frequently thought I recognised Theosophy in this. And that was well-known material for me. Moreover, in such situations I always think of the slogan `you can recognise the tree by its fruit'. I did not yet know them well enough, they told very little about themselves and their background, especially Vsevolod. And I got the impression that the other two were a little frightened of him. It was all far from beautiful. My family and friends believed I had entered a wasp's nest with my marriage to Georgy, and that my difficulties at the Sufi Circle had been superficial compared to this. They were very worried about me. And all this was still only the beginning of the `fun' with my Russian friends and my Georgian spouse… Through my marriage and Georgy's dependence on me and his dependence on them, I could not break with them immediately, so I remained involved with their activities for a while afterwards, initially more superficially. In spite of everything they had something attractive and captivating, they were more than those three macho Russian bears, who were like 'bulls in a China shop' …

I also had good times with them and their School and took part in several activities and foreign seminars, which were worth it. Vsevolod set himself up as a master of the Russian Christian hermeticism and also of alchemy. Elsewhere in this book I will explain this, since it concerns 'Faust in the twenty-first century'.

Vsevolod's main mission was and is, as I had recently come to understand, to indicate to humanity the possibility of a conscious contact and connection with the higher, spiritual worlds and the concept of spiritual freedom. This made me think of the message of Findhorn. It was the way of initiation, the way of the Golden Ladder, as Vsevolod called it, the way of Christianity. It was said that he was in contact with powers in the cosmos and I understood that these powers were interested in the spiritual evolution of mankind and of the entire cosmos. I had not been impressed, because due to the as yet unripe fruits, I had not got a really positive impression of the tree. But I was still interested in playing the game. Furthermore I knew, as a Theosopher, that an important task in spiritual growth is to learn to distinguish between what is true and what is not true, what is misdirection, and that is not at all easy! That requires a thorough training in the practice of daily living, preferably under the guidance of a master. We tend to believe everything in everyday life too quickly, especially if it sounds nice and if we feel safe, and especially if it is 'pleasant'. Truth and misdirection are frequently only separated by a hair's breadth and this makes things more difficult if you are in a search for God. There are innumerable side roads, that all seem equally attractive and especially good for our ego… My currency has always been: a healthy distrust and critical perception. If something is pure and true, I will know this immediately, I have learnt to trust this.

Kliment, a Cossack from the Caucasus, was the principal disciple of Vsevolod and Georgy, a Georgian, born in Kishinev, Moldavia, felt himself to be more a disciple of Kliment, because, as he told me, he found it difficult to handle Vsevolod's considerable energy and power. He felt himself thrown in at the deep end with Vsevolod whereas Kliment occupied himself with setting up a work programme for the disciples, so that they could cleanse themselves mentally and make peace with their past. That appealed to Georgy more. This difference between Vsevolod and Kliment had become evident in the course of time due to the way in which the disciples of both behaved themselves. Those who considered themselves as a disciple of Vsevolod, in the beginning were mainly Russians, were demonstratively close to him and had something arrogant about them, as if to say: `we are the chosen ones'. However, I have never noticed that they distinguished themselves from the others in any special way, apart from their consumption of much vodka and nocturnal parties with the master that lasted until morning. The only distinction I saw was in the way they looked down on the `lower' students. But everyone accepted that. Vsevolod had a mission and he had frequently referred Kliment and Georgy, during their trip, to the celebrated book `King Ape, travel to the west', the traditional Chinese epic of an adventurous pilgrimage, by Wu Ch'eng-ên. Vsevolod wanted them to read it meditatively, because they would find many similarities with living the lives that they led. `Study you previous incarnations attentively,' he repeatedly said, `this will answer many of your questions.' The monkey, said Vsevolod, was the prototype of Kliment and the pig the prototype of Georgy. For their mission Kliment and Georgy, under the guidance of Vsevolod who they considered as their master, travelled during the era of the Soviet regime for fifteen years, in Russia, Siberia, India and the areas in Asia which fell under the Soviet regime, such as among others Uzbekistan and Tajikistan. `Underground', as invisibly as possible, travelling in fear and angst for the KGB and betrayal, and regularly being involved with the Soviet Union. It was illegal to occupy yourself with spiritual matters, and many were sentenced to spend time in a mental hospital. People were frightened and for this reason distrusting and suspicious. Somewhere I read that Prof. Andrej Sacharov, the father of the soviet hydrogen bomb, said in an interview on Swedish radio that Soviet Russia was dominated by cynicism, apathy and exhaustion, pretence, decline of morality and of creative strength, as well as a decline in the intellectual population. And furthermore: that it would still take up to seventy years after the fall of the Soviet regime before the Russian people would recover mentally and spiritually, and would once again attain spiritual health.

A seminar in Latvia, which Georgy and I organised in May 1993, was the first international seminar that we organised for the School of Vsevolod and this, as I have already mentioned, met with a lot of resistance at the Sufi Circle. It was to be held at Toraida Castle in Latvia. And Georgy and I had discovered accidentally that a new airline company had been established, this being Lithuanian Airlines and that we would get large discounts on their first flight from Schiphol to Vilnius. Afterwards we would be transported with buses to Toraida and Kliment would organise that. It was so relaxed at this new airline that, when it occurred that one of our students forgot her passport and would be able to travel by means of a declaration from the customs authorities, the plane waited an hour for her. This was of course unique and it immediately put us all in a good mood. By means of a route suggested by Kliment we were driven by bus to Toraida after arrival in Vilnius and we passed among other things the mount of a thousand crosses, a revered holy place where everyone can plant a cross and make a wish, which is then fulfilled. There was a huge collection, as much as thousands, of crosses and it was impressive to wander around among them. The stay in Toraida was very special. The Latvians and Russians organised it so that the Dutch were comfortably housed in a hotel and they themselves stayed in small huts. For the Dutch separate food was cooked and served in a restaurant while they cooked their own food using electric cookers. But vodka made up for everything. On our arrival we were met by a couple of Latvians and Russians, who brought us to our rooms. Beside me was a nice Russian, and I wondered who he was, but we could not talk because I spoke no Russian. He proved be no less than my brother-in-law, Georgy's brother! I had of course never seen him. Our accommodation was in the vicinity of a river; in this a small sandy island on which we built a maze. We learned that we had to walk through this and recite a mantra and prayers and that we were then cleansed, to work for the most important task: obtaining cosmic conscience. This first seminar could be called pagan-hermetic. Kliment held lectures concerning Arcana Taro and accompanied the exercises in the maze. On the last day of the seminar a storm came up and we then saw the island disappearing under water … Only one pile, which we had planted in the middle on the island, continued to still protrude. It was an unforgettable seminar for everyone.

At the end of 1993 we were able by means of a friend of my mother, to rent a floor in the Speijkstraat. Initially Georgy and I had this floor rented to establish his professional life in the Netherlands, we had married in June and I was not planning to maintain him financially. Nobody would gain by that. A telephone was installed and Georgy decided to import wine from Moldavia, because his family lived there. Then Vsevolod and Kliment were in the Netherlands a couple of months later, and it soon became evident that they wanted to use rooms here for their meetings with interested parties. Everyone thought it was a good idea and Georgy and I agreed.

Then an interesting time began, which would last less than a year and in which Georgy and I organised all kinds of activities for the `Speijk Centre'. Vsevolod and Kliment stayed in the centre of Speijk from mid-1993 to mid-1994 and had their meetings there with mystics and other interested parties. I found it to be a really great, creative time. Georgy and I were enthusiastically busy with the founding of a successful activity centre. It succeeded very well and it flourished. I did this alongside my fulltime job as an administrator at an organisation, which was involved in a merger at that time, as a result of which I was very busy. The centre in Speijk was well visited, we made and printed the programme, had guest lecturers, Georgy did workshops concerning oriental healing techniques, all kinds of ways of predicting, tarot, Tibetan singing bowls (the loving wife promptly bought nine original singing bowls in support of this), and he held lectures concerning Gurdjieff and concerning the teachings of the Christian desert fathers. The centre was clearly developing. This went on for a number of months up to May 1994.

Now I must share something from the heart. Concerning 'powers in the universe' we always think immediately of something outside us. I have studied with interest the many gods, goddesses and saints of the various religions. In the Hindu faith I had been captivated for example by the role which all those perhaps many hundreds of gods and goddesses played in their daily lives. Also in Christianity there are a lot of pictures and images of saints and even of Christ. It is interesting that in icons the being of the saints is reflected and the icon painters, as well as the orthodox believers, believe and know that they meet the saint in a real and intimate way when praying to its icon. I once followed a debate on TV between a rabbi and a philosopher/atheist, who were presented as opposites. I was able to follow the arguments of both to the end and discovered to my surprise that they in fact said the same thing, but from a different viewpoint, differing in idea pattern and using a different terminology, as a result of which they found that they were on opposing paths. The interpretation of the scientist was materialistic and he referred to the genes in the brain, he proclaimed that there is even a God gene, which produces the religious persuasion in people and which, as he formulated it, keeps them 'fooled'. This is because it is just a chemical response, no more than that, in his opinion. The main objective of man, according to him, is evolution, by which he means material evolution. The rabbi disagreed with him in this and he claimed that the eventual aim is God. I thought: why is this not possible to observe by means of the so-called God gene?

It also occurred to me that the scientist was somewhat gaunt and dry: lack of spirituality? The rabbi gentler and more fluent: spiritual inspiration? My conclusion is, that people have everything within themselves but all in pictures, the complete cosmos, therefore also the concept of God, Jesus Christ, the saints, the gods and goddesses and so on. The material God gene? That certainly belongs there. People can coordinate those areas in themselves, and that is something I experience myself now, (if one wants to see it that way) and then have contact with that image, of God or a saint, or that god or goddess. Man is in fact all of those things himself! This sounds audacious, but it is simply truth in my opinion, it is our inner cosmos, the reflection of the external cosmos. At our stage of material and spiritual evolution we are, in terms of our concept of spiritual matter, still too limited to have access to this, but in the distant future this will be the reality for every individual: we are Adam Kadmon!

At the Theosophy group I had already become familiar with the 'White Lodge', with the Rishis and the Mahatmas, the great souls, that lead humanity on the ascending path to god. The teachings of Gurdjieff, who had contact with the Theosophy movement were, in the Russians' School, an indicator of a harmonious development and confrontation techniques, as psychological means, were regularly applied in the School. This last-mentioned was not 'my cup of tea', you had to have a strong solar plexus for that... Having had my first introduction to Gurdjieff at the home of engineer Ekkers some years ago, I now appreciated the friendship of Gurdjieff, after hearing his music in the United Kingdom and furthermore introducing his music at a house concert in the School. I found it very special, spiritual music. De Hartmann had written down this music, whereas Gurdjieff indicated the melody. It concerned the Asian Songs and Rhythms and Music of the Sayyids and the Dervishes. I also played his music at the Freemasons and thereby provided an explanation, which people found very interesting. Vsevolod made it clear that he was delighted with these developments. We also had a good teacher, Hein, who taught the Movements in the School, a type of movement teaching method which was created by Gurdjieff and gave a special, inner impact.

The School of the Russians in the Netherlands in those first years was quite hard and dynamic. Nowadays the environment seems to have become different, more neatly ordered and more targeted towards harmony and group consciousness, insofar as I see it. A rich social event has arisen, with the inevitable risk of fruitless 'consumption'. The programme and the activities are organised locally and make me think of the New Age. Sometimes a visit is organised a couple of times per year to the seminars in Russia and to meet Vsevolod and Kliment there, who now come once per year to the Netherlands. Then, in the beginning, it seemed that 'the end justifies the means'. I could appreciate the seriousness of this process from the point of view of the master, however, but I found the risk of major damage to be too great. Sometimes it seemed to me that a certain kind of sadism was involved. There was something capricious in the mutual relations, there was nothing wrong with unfaithfulness, just as with free sex, gossip did not matter because almost everyone was involved in it. One tried to be resistant against attacks and disappointments. We learned about our inner jamming station and our uroboros, psychological mechanisms that prevent our contact with the spiritual. Those were useful indications in the learning process. The master regulated the 'psychic temperature' in the School, which rose regularly, using alchemical means, whereupon a breeding ground for the solution of conflicts and problems arose. A lot of pain was suffered through our 'pain points', 'trauma buttons' and 'chips'; we had to learn to recognise these and render them harmless by struggling through the misery of the inner confrontation, whereupon we would see the light. This process was actually the epitome of pain. I have unfortunately never experienced an incident in which someone would put a loving arm around my shoulders during the endurance of the pain. That could in my opinion have had the most impact in the promotion of the catharsis...

These methods of esoteric instruction were in direct opposition to the Sufi teachings, with which I had been busy for many years, and which concerned `love, harmony and beauty', for `the fragrance or the soul', the transparency of the soul. I have described the disadvantage of striving towards such refinement elsewhere, and frequently meant ignoring one's own spiritual shadow, one's own negativity, the result being the well-known expedient of the projection of the shadow onto others and washing one's own hands in innocence. A `head in the sand' attitude, therefore.

I thought sometimes that, in the Catholic Church, confession was a very beautiful way for one to get to know one's own shadow and to subsequently experience forgiveness. Because we must get to know and use our shadow side!

Romance also had its turn. Vsevolod taught knighthood for a time, and gave instruction concerning the courtly, medieval court. We had to create a medieval court and function in it. He indicated that the higher worlds are not accessible for `peasant folk', that the development into the refinement of individuality is important for this reason. We all donned a sword and were crazy about films showing sword-fights. Courtliness and refinement did not receive much attention in the School, perhaps because there were more men than women in the School, whereas at the Sufi there were more women. The orientation towards culture was more present in the Sufi, there were artists and diplomats, and not forgetting: Inayat Khan himself, who was a major artist! Our three Russians were more like robust Russian farmers, determined, slightly coarse in their action, influenced by their Soviet context and their coarse experiences with the spirituality in Soviet Russia.

In his books Kliment tells about the `Russian mystic circles', where the mysticism was very special. In Russia this mysticism could take many forms: affectionate, inspiring, religious, rough, cruel, vodka, sinister drinking parties at graveyards etc. There seemed to be an affinity with the spirituality of the former, pantheistic Russia of pre-Christianity, which was just introduced in the year 1000 in Russia. A splendid tale is that of Prince Vladimir, who travelled around the year 1000 to Byzantium, to seek a suitable religion for Russia. He decided on Christianity, because this, as he defined it, is `the religion of beauty'. Promptly thousands of people were baptised in the river Dnjepr (or were decapitated if they did not want to, as I was told) and thus Christianity had gained a foothold in Russia. Russian people, with their large hearts, embraced Christianity, and Russian orthodoxy created a splendid mysticism around it.

Russia had no Renaissance and, unlike in Europe, there was no era of enlightenment. I found this to be very noticeable due to a certain superstition, or almost bigoted manner of experiencing their religion, whereby it is hardly relativised. I found that they tended towards considerable emotionalism, in the extreme, they take themselves very seriously. I had the impression, that 'individual thinking', critical thinking, the use of rationality, was not in line with their spirituality. Because that is a sin! It made me think of certain Christian Protestant groups in the Netherlands, whose strict sober teachings are well known and which are sometimes called `the black socks church'.

In all `teaching situations' in the groups at the School a warm group consciousness dominated, where much vodka was drunk, and where you could sink deliciously into forgetfulness and fantasy. Daily problems were then solved, communication problems no longer existed, love and affection received more of a chance, in short, life was your purest inspiration... This we know also from Russian literature. The inevitable hangover had now become legitimised, because the master had been in this 'situation' and we had in any case learnt a lot... I did not like this and was not often present in such situations, only in the beginning. I find that in the last couple of years a positive group consciousness has developed in the School. I remember that the teachers at the School attached great importance to this for various spiritual reasons and astral aims. Insofar as I understand it, this did not directly concern social aims, but situations in a distant future and in another world...

I have been confronted at very close range with all these traumas by my Russian friends and to no lesser extent by my Georgian (half Russian) husband. As a naive, innocent Western woman from a good background, I have thereby been confronted by some considerable traumas and it has taken me years to digest all of my anger and indignation. You could say, that I had, directly in Nigredo, reached the first stage of the alchemical process. I was one of the founders of the School in the Netherlands and could experience at close hand the inheritance of the Muscovite, mystic underground. I was a part of the very beginning of their Western adventure and have thus experienced certain things not known in the current School. It has taken me years to forgive them, but to forget is even more difficult. It has always been possible for me to live with Georgy, however, what else could I do? But that has meanwhile resolved itself and we recently celebrated our sixteenth anniversary.

The greatest illusion from which I had to free myself, after my experiences in the esoteric schools, is that you need someone outside yourself, in order to reach your spiritual home, God. On the contrary, the entire universe is within ourselves, and that is God, the Creator of all things. That process of getting to know oneself within continues and sometimes I can see through things in such a way that I wonder if I should not have become a hermit, somewhere in a remote hut. But then together with Georgy. After purification I would then only concern myself with transparency, with contact with the saints and doing useful things for my fellow men, such as book translations and writing...

Humanity as a 'horizontal' frame of reference is the greatest obstacle and at the same time the best exercise for our spiritual growth. That became clear at Vsevolod's School. We learn at a young age that the opinion of the outside world is important and to adapt accordingly. Thus the herd instinct arises, which was rejected by the Freemasons for example. That is the beginning of the path that leads away from God, you become increasingly less yourself, you lose contact with your true self more and more, you increasingly see things through a cloudy lens, in short, you become more 'horizontally' than 'vertically' focused, and the misery of horizontal life will be your lot and there is no escape. In my opinion it is a sin if you allow your inner self to be restricted by the ignorant outside world, whoever and whatever that may be. You become a distortion of the original image of who you are and I think that Christ came to help us restore this. Those who wish to follow the spiritual path must see through this and act accordingly, and that leads to a growing feeling of loneliness. Unfortunately and luckily.

This is, I thought, also the path the School is seeking, one trains oneself to acquire a sharpened perception by means of spiritual cleansing of the present, and especially of the past: reconsideration. This is a breathing and meditative technique which had been developed by Kliment, on the basis of techniques of the Tolteken, Taoïsts, Kriya and the spirit of the Christian tradition of the hesychasts. Another important exercise, that came later, was the prayer of forgiveness that we had to say regularly for everyone who played a role or had played a role in our lives and especially those with whom we were in conflict. I found these to be useful exercises, it helped. Kliment believed that the students underestimated how important these exercises were and that breathing and purification training formed the basis for spiritual growth: one should invest one's energy in this. The exercise of reconsideration, which he had set up, was a relatively simple breathing technique, with which the student could, in a systematic manner, 'illuminate' his past and subsequently distance himself from it. Many who practised this found that they profited from it, because when you cast off the pressure of the past you receive at last more room for the wide open future...
In May 1994 Georgy and I organised a seminar in the Ardennes and that was a great success. When we came back, I was so tired and drained that I said to Georgy one morning, before I went to

work that I was not able to organise the next seminar. Alongside my problematic fulltime job, I had entirely devoted myself to the 'van Speijk Centre' and to organising that seminar, but now I was totally exhausted from all the upheavals of the last months and my job. Georgy reacted in an extraordinary way. I had expected him to support me with sympathising and soothing words. But there was no question of it. He looked at me in a shocked manner, mumbled something that did not sound pleasant and disappeared, as I later discovered to the van Speijkstraat, where his friends were staying. What followed is incomprehensible to normal-thinking people. Years later the reason has become clear to me: fear of me, because they thought that I wanted to have power over them by means of the van Speijk centre, set up by Georgy and I. It is simply too ridiculous for words, and still crazier is their cruel aggression towards me, who had always been at their beck and call in every way. Idiot that I am. This was still a vestige of my Sufi-time, because they also wanted me, hard-working fool that I was, to do everything for them...

There was a members' meeting and Georgy proclaimed there in public, standing up in front of the meeting and supported by his two friends proclaiming that 'Maria only wanted power'. I was bursting with indignation, anger and tried to defend myself, but there little interest from the group. The visitors at the centre supposedly had no idea of all the work that Georgy and I had done together behind the scenes, and thought that if my husband said something like that, then it must be true. I decided to retaliate and immediately cancelled the lease of the van Speijkstraat centre that was in my name, because I had financed it. Later I heard that a meeting had taken place at Weltman's, an older student, where Vsevolod had demonstrated how Maria wanted to 'damage' the School in the Netherlands and that they had defended themselves. Wow, they must have been quite frightened of me ...

Although my 'friends' in the centre, the students, saw right under their noses what had happened there, they did not in any way come to my aid, even though they knew that I had no such underhand plans. The betrayal and the nonsense of people in the centre, who knew me well and who had been treated very well, was for me most incredible. I was betrayed on all sides. How I survived that year is still a puzzle and it is a miracle. I only slept with the aid of pills and alcohol, I performed increasingly badly at work and my thoughts were frequently in the clouds, but I continued to function somehow…

I was pursued with hatred and accusations by the Sufi Circle, the Russians, and at my work they tried to humiliate and belittle me, because they could smell blood. In the future fusion of three institutions three administrators had been involved, I being one of them, but there were only two necessary in the new organisation. I did not aspire to that position, because I wanted to take early retirement. But the two others, both men, could then, however, use their plots and backbiting to damage me and in this way secure their positions in the organisation. I do not believe that I was in a condition to show my best form. After the 'Van Speijk centre' had been closed, Else (also from the Sufi Circle) and my old friend Maud (from my work) and others found space in the Boreelstraat, not far from my house, note bene! Maud, a social worker in her thirties at my old employer, told me that she saw, however, what the Russians did to me, but that she could not openly support me, because she could no longer live without them. Vsevolod, Kliment and Georgy obviously also had such a major influence on her, that she had the feeling that she was no longer free. I have frequently said to people that a true master has a connection with his student that you can compare to an 8-likeloop, of which the junction of the lines between the two persons takes place. This indicates that there is no personal dependence. A master of the left hand path however is linked to his student by a 0 loop, therefore no junction of the lines. The student is caught, as it were, and a moment must come at which he must find the strength to free himself from this dependence, if he is indeed ever aware of it...

I no longer wanted to be married to Georgy and had already found a good lawyer, and had my demand for a divorce prepared and submitted and this was accepted. I had signed within six months, which was a grace of which the Russians knew, however, because if Georgy had to leave the country, this was also bad for their future plans. I felt so hunted by all the events, the pursuits and accusations, that I was in search of a refuge. I am not exaggerating, because I fought on three fronts: at my work I was pestered to the point of wanting to leave after the merger, at the Sufi I was the dog that had been kicked, because in their eyes I betrayed them by helping the Russians, and the Russians really beat everything with their outrageous plots. Georgy faithfully followed his two masters in this.

In my opinion I was confronted during my time with the Russians with such a shocking perversity, that it is almost inconceivable to me. During a deep, inner crisis I fell into an unfathomable, bottomless depth. But apparently I had not really lost and was helped by higher powers. During the deepest inner fall, it seemed that before I reached the bottom (and I do not know what that would have meant) I had been caught and my fall was interrupted. It seemed that the depth was shut off for me and I could not fall further. A floor had materialised.

In that time I had a creepy dream: I was walking in a pasture, in the direction of a caravan which was at the end of it and I had to meet my first spouse Andries and the Russians there. I went up the steps of the caravan and found a slimy, swampy situation there full of vermin, such as scorpions, spiders, snakes etc. I appeared to have a protective, transparent membrane around me, approximately 20 cm from my body. I was not frightened and felt safe and I walked around there quietly to look for them. Someone asked me what I was doing there and I answered by shrugging my shoulders. At a given moment there was a large black snake, thick as a boa constrictor, which slid up the outside of my membrane. I thought, gosh, how do I get rid of it and then I punched the snake hard against its head from the inside and it fell over. Its mouth fell open a little and it looked like Georgy's mouth... Just after this I dreamed I was somewhere in a house. I stood there and on the ground lay a human light being on his abdomen, bound with his hands on its back, the feet had also been bound. He could not move. I looked down at this light being and thought firstly 'leave him, let him lie there', but then suddenly I got a sort of shock and thought 'no, of course not, he must stand up!' and I also said that to the light being. That light being turned out to be me. I helped him stand up.

The black night that I went through was the experience that people with spiritual intentions manipulated in a hard-hearted, merciless manner in which the end justified the means and there was thereby an absence of every commiseration for the pain they inflicted on others. They walked all over people, because Vsevolod was pursuing an aim that was important for him and the innocent Sufi, as well as myself, were no equal to this. I realised, that all my efforts and good will were simply designed to help my spouse to gain a foothold in the Netherlands and to build a life here. He had to have work, have an income and an objective, and to this end I provided money and energy for the van Speijk centre. In May 1994, after the seminar in the Ardennes, organised by Georgy and I, which was a great success, I was very tired. The last day of the seminar the students thanked me (unexpectedly and at the last meeting) openly for my contribution to the organisation of this seminar, because without my commitment it would never have taken place. This seems to have been the breaking point for the Russians and Vsevolod, within the framework of his plans, obviously found that I had become far too 'powerful' and he didn't want that. And the 'fox in the bushes' knew what he had to do now. First destroy the marriage of Georgy and I, because this was a thorn in his side; and secondly: to bring me into discredit and make me submissive... In fact the whole thing would make you laugh, I was a wreck, anything but a pioneer, though I did admire Catharine the Great very much!

My adventure with the three Russians was therefore pretty serious in my life. It is clear that I had a karmic link with them, because I had immediately had a kind of 'recognition' with Vsevolod, whom I met in 1991, when he was with Kliment in the Netherlands. And that was entirely the case with Georgy. Kliment did not impress me much, I found him a bit creepy, he had something sultry and fanatical, something over-sexed. Vsevolod I took more seriously, although I have never considered him as someone to sway, in contrast to Georgy, because I 'knew' him. Vsevolod was the teacher of the two and that was fine. But not my teacher, I saw him as a friend, I did not trust him as a teacher. I had initially the impression that he was a Theosopher, and I knew something of that. He has the horoscope sign of Cancer, and I found him a typical example. My impression is that he had major spiritual qualities, and as a result could be very dangerous, if he was 'in the mood' for that. He knew how to play around with energies and create situations where nothing or nobody interests him except his aim. In the course of the years he has adapted to the Netherlands and now walks around like a kind of sphinx, with his favourite youngsters around him and in general seems somewhat less accessible than previously.

Vsevolod was born in the Soviet Union, in Moscow, in the forties of the previous century. He was brilliant, studied philosophy and psychology and was a student of some secret spiritual schools in Moscow. In the Soviet Union spirituality and religion had been prohibited and was even illegal. For this reason there were 'underground' movements of artists, philosophers and mystics that arose, where all manner of things took place and where Vsevolod was considered one of the spiritual founders. Many, nowadays well-known, Russian artists began their careers there. All kinds of things took place there, on the other hand, that could not be revealed. An actual anarchy dominated, because the situation was clandestine and highly secret, so that absolutely no structure existed. The mutual relations had been improvised hierarchically, and the power was held by those who acted most relentlessly and cruelly. As frequently occurred in Russia much, Vsevolod at the age of twenty already surrounded himself with interested parties, who called themselves his students and spent a lot of time with him. In such a group, some students disappear during the course of time and others remain. The groups were not large, about twenty or less. The mutual interaction in such a group was dynamic and targeted towards spiritual growth. Dynamically, because this process developed in a typical Russian manner, using vodka, tough confrontations, beautiful women (some students, some not), group travel, meetings with the followers of other spiritual trends and groups, such as arcanology, Fourth Way, Sufis, anthroposophy, teachings of Castaneda, shamanism etc.

Kliment was born in the fifties in the Caucasus, he was Cossack. At thirty he met Vsevolod and recognised in him his teacher. After some time he became Vsevolod's most important disciple. He was already occupied with meditation at a very young age and sought contact with spiritual teachers. Especially the Indian guru Yukteshwar was important to him. By profession he was a computer programmer.

Georgy, the youngest of the three, was a different case. After high school he studied theoretical physics. Although he graduated in this, he himself has never understood why he had chosen that course of study. He was extremely intelligent, intuitively and artistically gifted. The gentlemen are all three extremely intellectual and advanced in Russian and European literature for example. Georgy behaved like an opportunist. He found in Kliment his spiritual teacher and a year later they both became disciples of Vsevolod. He took part in the hectic life style of their tours in the Soviet Union with a jazz band, for which they performed the technical work. Spiritual living was taboo in the Soviet Union and so during those trips nothing could be revealed of it, otherwise you could end up sometimes in a mental institution.

These events would later be described in the books of Kliment concerning the Russian mystic circles. In these books Vsevolod's mission as spiritual teacher and messenger was discussed as well as how Kliment and Georgy accompanied him as his students and shared a lot of very difficult experiences and circumstances. It is the coarse tale of an immensely large country, Russia, the former Soviet Union, the traumatic life of its occupants under the soviet regime, especially the fear of the authorities, KGB and each other, the fear of betrayal. This society will need years to overcome a lot of the trauma incurred.

* * *

CHAPTER 7. THE THREE RUSSIANS: MORE CONCERNING THEIR TEACHINGS AND THEIR SPIRITUAL BACKGROUND

Kliment gives a report in his books of the experiences of the last twenty years of the previous century of the School and its relationship to Christianity. In these reports the line of inner initiations can be followed, which should lead inch by inch and by means of transformation to the highest initiation, unity with the divine. Specific terms are used, such as `striving towards reaching the Heavens' and terms from the alchemist, such as inner gold, nigredo, albedo etc. On the path to realisation or indeed `the path to Heaven', that this School in Russia followed, inner, spiritual and psychic processes occurred in everyday life at the time of the Soviet Union and accompanied the consumption of a lot of vodka, cooked chicken, onions and sausages. Those Russian underground, mystic circles are unknown to the west. There were artists, curious citizens, mystics, philosophers who wanted no part of the dominating culture (socialist realism) and the materialistic ideology. An alchemical master was seen as an inspiration to the core group, who felt it their duty to pass on mystical inspiration in the form of literature and fine art. This underground movement can be considered as the `purgatory' of spiritual life at that time. In these circles the psyche, the spirit, matter all boiled up and all phases of decadence were represented, but also that of renewal in art and culture. Here the extremes met each other. The master alchemist considered these underground movements as an excellent, school of hard knocks for his students. A running theme throughout the books of Kliment were the teachings of the master alchemist and the splendid concept of the contact with the `Ray of Paracletus', the inspirational source of their mysticism and the advance of their School. The concept of `ethereal initiation', the meeting with our highest self, was new for me. What I found important in the books was the solidarity of the School with Christianity. Mysticism, and with that the devotional orientation of the student during the learning process, can prevent his fall into the world of Mephistopheles. In his journey to Heaven, the steep Path upwards, the student encounters a lot of side paths, which seem extremely tempting, especially that of the intellectual knowledge aspect or psychisms.

Vsevolod considered himself a messenger from the era of the Paracletus, of spiritual freedom. I think the actual spiritual development of the three Russians in fact started in the Netherlands, in the case of Vsevolod perhaps this concerned the form in which he poured out his message, but for Kliment and Georgy this is certainly the case! I initially found them to be rather 'coarse' material that had to be treated and from which just about anything could originate. Their feeling of self-importance was however frequently considered out of proportion by many. Their ideals were also magnanimous: the west had to be converted! They had no idea whatsoever about what had happened on a spiritual level in the west since the sixties of the previous century or the developments that have taken place there. But I only had to refer to the Findhorn Community or the innumerable esoteric schools, such as the Theosophy movement, Sufism, Anthroposophy and others. They had been brain-washed by the Soviets to believe how bad and stupid the west was, however, and for this reason they came to convert us and, more interestingly still, take us to distant, perhaps astral, aims. Georgy told me that Vsevolod gave them a very intensive training during their travels through Russia. Vsevolod had his own vision about what the Sufis call 'teaching stories', stories containing transcendental wisdom. He told Kliment and Georgy these stories, together with his extensive comments, during their travels, and they used the information as study material. One of the key tales for someone who wanted to follow the spiritual path according to Vsevolod was the tale of Maarouf the shoemaker from the 'Thousand and One Nights'.
He had a vision that the three of them, after the communist period, would bring his spiritual message to the west, therefore they had

to follow an education. And the most important property that they had to develop was an inner, positive contact between the three of them, irrespective of distance and time, life and death. Vsevolod called it `alchemical fusion'. After many years of extremely painful ordeals they had developed this contact. But in the beginning, for some years, Georgy and Kliment could not believe all of that and according to Georgy's stories, they always had to laugh about that: because that was nevertheless inconceivable! The circumstances were totally contrary to these beautiful stories: frequently Vsevolod shared his splendid visions with them, while they dragged two tons of equipment from the jazz band, somewhere in a godforsaken town in the middle of the vast Soviet Union. Vsevolod illustrated this with the picture of the Tang monk, Sun Wukong and Zhu Bajie from the renowned novel `Monkey: journey to the West' by Wu Cheng'en. He prepared and coached them from 1983 up to approximately 1994 during their travels. They learnt to strengthen their characters through confrontations and difficult experiences, they learned how to handle people, and especially how they could gain access to things, because that was important for the contacts and the distribution of the teachings. Their practise arena concerned women, of course, artist circles, and especially the Moscow and Peterburg mystic circles. This was not always easy, and the survival of the fittest applied, in every area, however. They learned how to gain `access' to both groups and individuals, how they could put pressure on people, they brought food with them on their first visits and cooked for their hosts, all this in order to find favour and perhaps win followers. A part of the training concerned cooking, cleaning and carrying out small domestic tasks, Vsevolod called it the `school of Vanjka Zhoekov', after the story by Chekhov. This concerns a poor orphan called Vanjka Zhoekov from a village, who was placed as an apprentice with a shoemaker. According to Georgy everyone who wanted to become a student of Vsevolod noticed, sooner or later, that in the company of Vsevolod he assumed the role of Vanjka Zhoekov, irrespective of the position he held in 'normal' life. Some, however, had finished this 'school' rapidly, but others stayed around for years there... This whole educational situation was referred to by Vsevolod, Kliment and Georgy as 'chess', by this they meant: in the communication process 'to be able to play chess', that they would always achieve their aim and get what they wanted. They practised this especially on women, of course, and success was assured... Georgy was indeed a strong 'chess player', I felt. If something came into his head, then he found all the necessary ways and means to achieve it, both lawful and unlawful... Yes, that was perhaps not the best way, but was effective in handling those barbaric, rough circles in Russia, at least that's the way I see it. I saw that Georgy also had certain properties that I envied, such as the ability to let go internally of what people do or say to you, or if they want to hurt you. He could shake that off easily. But I found that he had also incurred physical and mental damage over time. Physically, due to the heavy load that he and also Kliment, had to carry, together with Vsevolod, when working with the jazz band, and mentally due to the fear of the police force and KGB. Georgy admitted to being a major skirt chaser at that time and looked back with little pride.

In the Netherlands, after 1994, there were new developments and Vsevolod let his two students go. He concentrated now on new students and Kliment and Georgy had had to try in their own ways to give form to the message of the School and to discover what roles they can play in this. Their original agreement, that the three of them would spread the message of Vsevolod, was something they still complied with however.

After their arrival in the Netherlands Georgy started taking life seriously. He had to, however, because it appeared he had to start all over again with his social development, in order to handle living in the Netherlands. He had in his youth completed a university course in theoretical physics in Kishinev, but he did not want to do anything further with this. He had to learn to speak fluent Dutch, but also English. I helped him with this as much as possible. He needed some years for his development, years that were also not easy for me. But his considerable intelligence helped him follow several training courses successfully, such as bookkeeping, management, data processing, computer programming, he also obtained the intermediate diploma, and looked for a way of earning money. In Russia he had from time to time done some painting jobs and work on houses, which he took up here and knew how to develop that into a rather competitive company, which delivered skilled work. As a publisher he also had a lot of success.

If I look back to that initial time, in the nineties, I regret that I did not act more powerfully, and defend myself more powerfully against the Russians and the Sufi Circle. Perhaps I did that but I myself went under. I was sick of all those dreadful events and thought of only one thing 'I want rest'. Because my work and also my private life was a mess in those years and I was pursued and accused. The worst that happened was that my integrity was in doubt. My honour was severely damaged. An astrologer explained to me later that the planets in my horoscope clearly indicated these events, using the image of a traffic roundabout where cars come from all sides at the same time. Consequence: chaos and damage...

Then a new phase started for me. I started by asking myself what use it had to be a member of an esoteric group or school, what could this add to my quest for the goal which I had set for myself: to become aware of true life, of love, of my fellow men, of my deepest being... I thought of the 'Know Thyself' above the door of the temple in Delphi, to the place of the priestess, the pythia, where I travelled during my time in Greece, at the beginning of the eighties, and had sat and meditated. There were no sulphur fumes coming from the depths, but I experienced a vague identification with her... I realised myself that I had become too dependent on the standards, the approval and the acceptance of hierarchies and members of certain organisations. Of course there, in a spiritually specific organisation, a relationship between teacher(s) and student exists, where the student opens himself (temporarily) and delivers himself in faith to the knowledge and the power of the teacher (s). In India this relationship between guru and chela is even holy and yet very ordinary. It is a very serious relationship and it even happens that the chela, the student, identifies himself with his guru to such an extent that it seems that he eventually completely `forgets' himself. At a given moment he even thinks, speaks and acts like his guru.

Once when I attended the School meeting something funny happened that seems to illustrate the guru-chela relationship: Georgy and I walked from the lake to the road, where the hotel stood. In the distance I saw Vsevolod standing, with someone else. I thought it fortunate that he had arrived, because he had problems with his visa and was not there yet. Then we approached and I saw that it was not Vsevolod, but Kliment who stood there. I greeted the group and said to Kliment: `I thought that you were Vsevolod' and then Kliment said that this was a coincidence because he had just received an `astral message' from Vsevolod. He was, therefore, in a certain way still in connection with Vsevolod and I had therefore observed that. Perhaps it was also a manifestation of their `alchemical fusion', about which Vsevolod had spoken? The following night I dreamt I was in a mountainous area and suddenly Vsevolod, Kliment and Georgy came walking towards me. They smiled as they passed by me and I noticed that all three had exactly the same eyes: large and almond-shaped, with a pale brown colour and a beautiful expression.

Returning to the subject of identification with the guru: this did not attract me, I felt myself to be a Western woman, although India had always made me feel `at home'. I have certainly had splendid lives there. I saw such a symbiotic relationship between master and student happen in certain Russian students of Vsevolod. I cannot remember encountering this phenomenon in the Netherlands, except perhaps in students of one of the Sufi sheiks? In the Far East such a relationship is considered the most important path to enlightenment. But as a westerner I realised that Europe had experienced a time of Renaissance and Enlightenment and restored the use of and respect for independent thinking, independent judgement, after the major power which the church had exercised over people. Then, at the end of the Middle Ages, this meant the end of the (especially psychological) power of the church concerning the believers. This was supported by the development of book-printing and the familiarisation with new spiritual and cultural movements from other parts of the world, especially from the Islamic world. I had a strong freedom compulsion and could not in the long run allow my own freedom to be denied.

Later it appeared that the development of the notion of my own responsibility was a prime mover in clearing the way to within, to my own inner self, the way to God. Because, although I saw myself as a Sufi and mystic, it was clear that the path to God can be compared to the mystic tale of the knights of the Holy Grail, who had to put up such a fight. The knighthood, the inner warriorship, of the seeker of God, are indispensable. I remember that Vsevolod in the first years of their Christian-hermetic School in the Netherlands referred to life at the medieval court, to the courtly and brave knights, the reserved noble ladies, in short: towards the importance of inner and external nobility. Perhaps my attitude to the outside world seemed stubborn, but I could not and would not do otherwise. I refused in a certain way to comply with the standards and regulations of social living, the 'horizontal' life. The conflict with the Sufi Circle forced me to face the fact that I had a right to find my own way and live life in my own manner, as long as I did not bother or wish to bother anyone. This concept was confirmed textually by freemasonry. I started to realise that at this stage of my life I had to undergo a learning process, a kind of ` do or die', that I had to realise my restrictions and discover that outside the maze of my personal live, another and larger life existed: the cosmos, and that I was a part of it. I had not yet got as far as this, when I realised that this purely concerned inner life. I did not know yet that it would be a painful process and that the confrontations with myself would indeed mean `do or die'. I had not yet heard much of Gurdjieff, the Russian spiritual teacher and knew nothing of his hard approach towards his students. Gurdjieff was an important teacher in the School of Vsevolod and was frequently cited. His hard method has been aimed, so that the `horizontal' (in contrast to `vertical', spiritually) thinking became disoriented and as a result makes the access to a higher consciousness possible. The growth after these confrontations is considered to be a transformation of consciousness.

I was aware that I was bound in a `sticky' way to the influences of the outside world, to the opinion and approval of others, that I did not know who I was, in spite of my spiritual activities. I lived vulnerably, anxiously and uncertainly. Not so much that the outside world noticed this, that prevented the lion on my ascendant, but my inner lens was clouded. In the education of my generation we were imprinted to think that the outside world is always right, and that we ourselves are always wrong, this was considered the key to acquiring the grace of the other `ignorant parties', and this you would live to influence favourably and then you would have success. It is unbelievable that I have been stuck in this way for so long, but that seems to belong to my generation. Recently I read, to my delight, in a splendid book about a Russian saint, that when everyone likes you, you can assume that you are on the wrong path, because then you neglect to do God's will. This saint considered it a favourable sign if the outside world does not like you because then the chance is that you have an honest and good contact with God. Gradually I have discovered how wise this saint was. I grew towards the notion of inner freedom, where you have purified thinking with much effort from the overwhelming influences of the outside world. This I realised for the first time at the aura and chakra healing training, and had tried by means of given techniques. Therefore this spiritual purification must firstly take place before you obtain your inner space, your inner clarity and then you can start the adventure, the

exploration of living above and below, and the search for God. That the adventure of your own creativity, your own initiatives is based on your conditions and vision and not those of other people...
This can mean that you detach yourself (inwardly and outwardly) from your surroundings, and follow your own path. Spiritual organisations have a temporary usefulness, but then the moment must come when you yourself take responsibility for your life. An organisation needs people to continue to exist and to spread their good message. You are welcome as an element of that whole and that is fine, however, if you realise that and you are not misled by massive promises and expectations, and especially that you are something special!! In my case I was easily seduced, because I was also still sensitive to flattery, the characteristic of my lack of self-knowledge, by which I have practical qualities and people therefore gladly used me...
Sometimes flattery goes so far, that you will think that you can share a great spiritual secret, and that you belong to the few chosen ones...!

I was, through my Theosophical study, sensitive to the motto `serve your fellow man'. This was my ideal, but I had to discover what I in fact had to offer humanity!

I followed the path of transformation. That happened fairly unconsciously and there were many, almost insuperably painful barriers. The Russians would play a role, whether or not I wanted to admit it. I was to choose the path of confrontations, hate, choices, painful self-knowledge, love between man and woman, `go with the flow', which is uncontrollable and full of creative energy and still much more.

* * *

Chapter 8. The Freemasons

Then, in August 1994, when I was in the middle of nigredo (alchemical purgatory), suddenly an idea occurred to me, that originated from outside, because I had never thought of it. I received a suggestion to get in touch with the Freemasons, to connect with them thereby and this way to find a free place and practical and spiritual protection in my current situation. I took the telephone book and rang a lady who was mentioned in this as a member of a mixed Freemason lodge, Mrs J. Van der Wolkoff. She lived near me. We made an appointment and I was introduced at the mixed Lodge Plotinus. After all kinds of formalities I was initiated on 10 January 1995 an Entered Apprentice, on 28 May 1996 (the birthday of my father, who in the then Dutch Indies had also been a Freemason) passed to the degree of Fellow Craft and on 23 September 1997 after taking the test, was raised, as it is called, to Master Mason.

It was done according to the Scottish Ritual. I rapidly became acquainted with rituals and symbols and already fulfilled the function of secretary of the lodge. As a workaholic, I always enjoy doing useful work, and continued to embroider on the badge that I got when I was a girl scout (I was then a gnome and approximately twelve years old). The yellow ribbon of 'helper'. That suited me well, because my whole life long I had this compulsion, almost unconsciously, to help. Sometimes with not such pleasant results, because before you know it you are in a kind of centre of events, which you had not intended. That time in freemasonry has been very important for me. I had great respect for the life style which was pursued, the civilisation of our culture, the civilised and respectful manner with which they treat each other, in short: pursuing inner nobility. We wore sober black-and-white clothing: long black skirt, white blouse, no jewellery. The men were in smokings.

The Freemason is expected to free himself from the herd spirit in society and to realise that it is about himself/herself, that he/she stipulates his/her life path to be followed. He must find his own individuality. There, however, a hierarchy existed in the form of three degrees and functions, but this was no longer than logically thereby be able to perform the work. The meaning and contents of these ranks were clear for everyone and reaching a higher degree was everybody's own choice and responsibility. This attracted me very much. We learned, that you become more and more able to make a positive contribution to society by means of inner growth. Because that is the aim of freemasonry, of bringing the world in line with a higher plan. The rituals had been aimed at the individual realisation process and reflected the history of freemasonry, returning to ancient Egypt, the Templars and the Jewish-Christian tradition. I found the rituals and ceremonies really splendid, yet did not understand them fully for a long time. And I was not alone in this, because in the lodge it was frequently put simply that, although misunderstood, the rituals of the freemasonry in the current form must be passed on entirely intact to the following generations, and there will come a time that one will know their meaning and that their role in the development of humanity will be clear. Later I discovered that the rituals concern, in fact, the Christian mystical initiation process and are also intended to do so. The aim was to remove individuality, to become aware of brotherhood, in the first place the brotherhood of the Freemasons. I still use, in practical life, the knowledge that I acquired, I understand situations better and can afterwards integrate them in a fertile manner into the course that my life is taking. Especially the teachings of the three degrees: Apprentice, Fellow Craft and Master Mason, which also applied in the medieval guilds, are an inspiring directive for my life. Practically, but also ethically or aesthetically.

After seven years of being a Freemason, I got the feeling that I had not progressed much spiritually and that I focused too much on the formal, because that is also a certain learning aspect. I found the meetings similar to each other and I wondered whether I was really growing or if I just enjoyed it all as an ordinary social activity. As with the earlier Templars there was an enjoyable social life in the lodges, there were celebrations and the organisation was neatly organised and clear. I have really learnt an awful lot and consider myself a real Freemason. That is a good feeling. It has to do with the striving towards inner aristocracy, discipline of oneself, the brotherhood, individuality of character and no herd instinct, social feeling and idealism. I assumed that I had returned to the lodge enough for its welcoming and protecting accommodation, which I had found there, when I really needed that back in 1994. I have been a conscientious secretary, according to some sisters even somewhat too dutiful… In 2001, I announced that I wanted to take a year's 'break', and that I did not yet know if I would come back afterwards. I had been a member of Plotinus Lodge for seven years.

Vision concerning the cobra.

In that period I wanted make myself useful again as a Freemason for humanity by becoming a governing board member of a charity. At least I thought that.
I had agreed to the explicit request of a Dutch woman, who lived in India, and after she had begged insistently, eventually agreed to be the secretary/treasurer of a yet to be set up foundation, that would channel Dutch donations to India. It was for a good purpose: her orphanage for poor children. I tackled the work in my well-known transparent manner, with the consequence that I became less and less popular with her, because she proved to have no need for transparency. After I had been in India with two colleague governing board members, with whom I got on well, to examine the project, I stepped down as member of the foundation. On the location of the orphanage, near Tiruvannamalai (the former place of residence of Ramana Maharshi) there were, it was said, rather a lot of snakes, especially cobra.

When I was back in the Netherlands, I had a type of vision or experience, where suddenly, while I was sitting on the ground, in the half darkness, I 'saw' a large cobra approaching. Near me she raised herself and opened her hood. I was numb with fear and also full of admiration, because I thought she was really beautiful. We stared at each other for a few seconds, and somehow I then suddenly said `I am innocent', I do not know why I said that, but I had to say it. That proved to be good, because then she left. Since that time I am less frightened of snakes. I have now and then told the story of this vision and had some very beautiful answers, concerning my subconscious. Georgy related the vision however to the animosity of this lady and her Indian consorts, who profited financially from her and probably saw in me a threat... That was therefore a dream/vision concerning a snake in conflict situation.

After that year, when I was busy with a number of other matters, I made the mistake, on the insistence of the chairing master concerned, who was a friend of mine, to let myself be persuaded to join another lodge. That was a lodge, where the English Ritual was carried out and that was different from the Scottish Ritual. Later I understood that they had a shortage of master Freemasons for the rituals and it is of course legitimate that they tried to get me in. My health was not good at that time, because in south Russia, in the Crimea, I had contracted a persistent pneumonia, which was not recognised firstly and which cost me a lot of energy. At a given moment I thought the end of my life was in sight, I was so limp and weak. Therefore I was not at my best. After a personal conflict with someone at the lodge, who accused me of `dominating' when I made a joke, I decided to leave the lodge. That was in 2003. Presently I do not intend to submit an application at a lodge. But I see it as an honour to be a Freemason.

I have been bound to the oath, that I may tell nothing concerning the contents of freemasonry and I remain faithful to that. I made several Builder's pieces. These are important study assignments or pieces of work, as a type of examination, for access to a higher degree. They are presented as lectures in the lodge, and also in the other lodges. From these it should appear how your inner development has progressed and if you are ripe enough for the next initiation. My assignment for the third initiation, the master initiation, concerned `painting icons' and I described my experience of learning to paint my first icon.

In February 1997 our life changed and a new, splendid chapter in the life of Georgy and I started, the impact of which can still be felt until now (June 2009). By means of a nun that knew Georgy, we were made aware of an icon course by Bernard Frinking, a student of icon painter Leonid Ouspensky from Paris, who belongs to the tradition of only passing on knowledge and skills orally. There I received a number of insights, with which I have occupied myself intensively in the years afterwards. It was a ten-day orthodox study, wherein fifteen of us lived at that time in the church in Amsterdam and followed the way of life and church services as in a convent. We learned that painting an icon requires an in-depth preparation. First of all: by means of prayer or meditation reaching inner silence. Then the 'fasting' of eyes, ears and mouth. We discovered by means of a drawing experiment that we cannot really see, because we do not really 'see' the seen but we learn to 'think' it. Concerning the ritmogram that is the external form and reproduction of the inner self of the saint that we learnt to paint in one pen-stroke! Because we had to get to grips with the inner state of the saint and feel that environment within ourselves. Then we had to learn the exact geometrical proportions (the laws), to know how - according to the tradition - the face and the body of the saint had to be reflected. At the catechism, at night, we learned about the consignment of people, and that the way of Christ was a therapeutic path, healing. From what do we have to heal? From death.

Icon painting is the Way of the Heart.
During the course I went inwardly through several confrontations and pain (my past, my fears, certain blockades) and I felt as if I had come internally under increasing pressure. On the sixth day it was so difficult for me, that I grabbed my coat and went outside. I walked for a couple of hours along the Amsterdam canals and then sat on a bench. Inwardly the pressure was still there, also a certain despair, and suddenly I felt tears. I did not cry, because I could never do that well, but nevertheless the tears flowed down my face. After some time I returned to the church building, where we stayed and studied for these ten days. When I related my experience, a little astonished, to someone, I was embraced and was congratulated, because it was considered 'a moment of purification of the lower nature', a moment of mercy. I became gradually conscious of growing an inner dimension, behind the dimension that I knew already

from my intellectual and spiritual quests. During a liturgy I saw in a vision that I had to jump over a type of abyss to enter a new dimension, a dimension of light that gave a totally new vision of who we are on this earth, on the endless cosmos. The space and light which I saw on the other side of that abyss is not accessible by means of the study of our existing knowledge or theology in whatever form, nor with the resources of our senses and our understanding. By means of the vision of this new dimension, I became conscious of enormous possibilities and panoramas (also for the intelligence!) and (for me) new laws regarding Man and the Cosmos. That the way of knowledge is possible by means of revelation, the spiritual life. Georgy and I still followed some courses of this icon painter afterwards, and it appeared that Georgy had a great talent for painting icons. After painting an icon of the Saint George he was blessed especially by the archbishop and he worked for some time as an icon painter for the church. A number of his icons are hanging there. I was less skilful with the brush and gave lectures concerning the superb inner process that we had experienced. Those ten days in which we had lived and worked in the church were an intense experience for us both and my eyes were opened to the depth of Christianity. In March 1997 I was promptly anointed in the Russian Orthodox Church of Mary Magdalene in The Hague. I had already been baptised in Indonesia shortly after my birth in the Catholic hospital, therefore anointment with oil was now sufficient, the Russian priest found.

Many Freemasons are not much interested in the Christian church, but nevertheless listened with interest to my assignment, especially in the higher degrees. Afterwards they said they were glad to know something more concerning the context and the meaning of icons and would examine them now in a new light. The brothers and sisters of my Lodge Plotinus were intellectually focused, business-like, no-nonsense, which I generally appreciate very much.

I have been a member for seven years of the mixed Freemason Plotinus lodge and consider this period as a very useful and beautiful experience. In one way or another the experience with the Freemasons was not as 'loaded' as my experience with the Sufi, the Theosophists or the Russians. I think back gratefully to this period, to my sisters and brothers, and to the experience which I have gained, but the impression left behind is less indelible. There were many ceremonies, it was formal, and after the lodge always extremely sociable. However, I could no longer muster up the patience at a given moment to sit out all the rituals, which did not always go smoothly, because nobody knew the rituals by heart. I did not get the impression that one changed very much personally, which is nevertheless the intention of the personal development as Freemason. Perhaps the external aspects, the decorum and the trappings of freemasonry distracted me from the inner task? It was pleasant to make contacts, sometimes they became friends, and were generally people `of class', intellectually and socially. I did not think that the older school was open to a lot of change. My relation with the chairing master deteriorated after a couple of years, supposedly because I did not wish to introduce her at the meetings with the Russians. She knew my situation with Georgy and the other two Russians and I had told her about the pluses and minuses, and she had been interested, but I was frightened that, if the meeting did not go well I would have problems. That was the last thing I needed. At that time my relationship with the Russians was a terrible mess and I was in the middle of trying to repair my marriage. I consider the seven years at the Freemasons as a time in which I had found an urgently needed niche, a safe accommodation for protection against those who thought to slander me in first half of the nineties. And that `niche' is something for which I will always be very grateful.

***

Chapter 9. Contemplations

Gradually I became aware that schools, their teachings and their masters are in themselves very good, and that these external situations were, however, instructive, did not bring me any closer to myself, or to God. I had the feeling that they, generally with the best of intentions, wanted to imprint their soul on me, and that my soul, the most inner part of me, was being suppressed. I had no image of this or that. I only knew that if I had withdrawn from the external teachers I would have come into my own `universe', and would have found myself among a Family, which is vaguely comparable with the presence of angels, higher figures, Jesus Christ, perhaps God. I had a vague notion of what I expected of them, but always thought that they would manifest themselves, however, by means of external situations. Vsevolod said once to me, that they (or only he, I no longer know which) belong to the White Lodge. I took a great interest in this.

I still always sought a school, an external school, but still always failed and returned to my isolation. As I did not yet know how I would find this path within myself (the true inner school?) definitively I sought solace and information in the outside world, at schools and spiritual organisations. I met nice friends, who were also in search and that was comforting.

At this moment I know that my meeting with Orthodox Christianity, therefore with the Russian Orthodox Church has brought me eventually to my desired path. Thus, after my meeting with the Russians and their School. Vsevolod once said that my intuition was developed and that I should trust that.

This can be illustrated as follows:
In translating the books of Kliment I frequently encountered words and expressions, which I 'heard' later `coincidentally' during my prayers and in my meditation, once during my contact with Saint

Panteleimon. This week it was very clear with respect to the term Kliment defined as `the mystic crystal', that we must form within us and that gives us strength and the direction to grow. During a meditation I asked Saint Panteleimon my question concerning this term, and then he indicated to me a spark within myself, something that shines, and he said that it only concerns this spark, and nothing else, also nothing that happens to you in the outside world. He referred to this core as most important and that I should remember this.

Another word from a book of his is the `wind' of the School and description of it.

On 25 February 2002, very early in the morning, I had a marvellous vision and then I sat behind my computer with my eyes closed, so as not to be distracted, and wrote the poetical prose below. I did not know what this wind was and Vsevolod had the poem read aloud a week later, translated into Russian, during a meeting.

> *I feel the breath of the wind from behind the curtain*
> *It comes from a distant past, from a faraway place and time*
> *It was there always, it blows without stopping through planets and stars*
> *Borders do not exist for wind, it blows for centuries and centuries*
> *Wind is clear as a crystal and has a golden brilliance, it carries love with it...*
> *Down through the ages it carries the message to humanity: the divine will appear on earth*
> *The forms in our world give accommodation to wind and they awaken*
> *And know that they are expected, somewhere at the borders of worlds*
> *The wind of the Holy Spirit is there since the creation of Adam*

And that enabled the Holy Spirit to incarnate in millions of people.
This always happened, it happens even now
By means of ideas and feelings, poetry and the music of the spheres
By means of faith, hope and love, by means of the harmony of the spirit
The ray of help from the higher worlds occurs by means of the sacrifice of the bearers of the wind
Wind always blows, it is as eternal as the law of beauty
We do not know from whence it comes and where it goes
It is the wind of the Holy Spirit, the wind of the God already existing
The wind of celestial valleys of golden brilliance
Brilliance that is always present in the depth of man
And awakens him to universal consciousness
So that he changes from a cosmic point to a massive sphere
In a sphere which will inflame once and become a star
That is the spiritual person.

I find here a consistency with the very spiritual text of Inayat Khan, Nasihat, intended for meditation, which I mentioned earlier in this book.

Sometimes I had a funny dream: I dreamt that I did breathing exercises, on a chair, with two people from the School. I had been challenged and they wanted to see if I could do it. Opposite me sat Harmen. I started vigorously with the exercises, and began to inhale and exhale in a certain manner. But immediately my face began to twist and to swell, my left eye was squeezed shut by a swelling and I was astonished. But I did not want to give up, therefore I simply continued. A little later I said that I would stop and then the dream ended. Georgy said this morning that those exercises were obviously not intended for me.

Today is my mothers ninety-ninth birthday... We have prayed since her death very regularly for her and in the Russian Orthodox church we ask the priest to hold office for the dead for her on special occasions, which are special prayer services for the deceased. Her name thus remains always in the commemoration book for the deceased family members, that Georgy gave the priest every Sunday and she is prayed for there, also for my father. We know that this is important and a spiritual support for the deceased. Their souls then receive a pulse of light and divine love, and that can help them further in the state in which they find themselves. I do not think frequently of my mother, I think that in the last years before her death too many bitter things had happened. I think that she also wrestled with her experiences in her youth, the experience of the Japanese camp, the death of my father, and that this had become more serious in her old age. If one by that time has made no effort to do something, such as reflection, forgiveness, self-forgiveness, and praying to Jesus Christ, regarding these memories of the past, then they will grow as a weed and eventually be expressed in an uncontrolled way. Especially due to projections and these then become a hell... And certainly for those around you...

I have no portrait of her in my house, however, only of my father. Straight after I became owner of the house and I acquired two young tenants on the ground floor through my piano teacher. They asked me if they could demolish the closets and put in new floorboards and remove the rug in the corridor, to which I agreed. At night in bed, I felt a heavy, very panicky feeling, something like `they are busy demolishing the house, do something! I resisted the pressure, thinking `well, so what?' Later I thought that it must have been Thea, as we called my mother. She was always sober and realistic and it was quite possible that she had provided me with this insight from beyond the grave. Afterwards I dreamt that we were walking beside each other, with a couple of other people, and that I said expressly to her: `The house is now mine!'
I meant with that, that she shouldn't interfere any longer. She was okay with that.
Then I dreamt once that I visited her in a hospital, she lay there in bed with nurses around her. It was not clear to me what illness she had. Once I dreamt that I met her on the street, she was a young woman in her early twenties. I was also around twenty and we were studying at the university. We encountered each other and I greeted her as a good friend, and she me. After this I rarely dreamt of her.
I am Christian with strong bonds to the Russian Orthodox Church. It gives me a lot, it gives me direction for the path to the light, for the higher aspects in me, so that in the fight for life I have a direction I can recognise. I have tended to give myself over to the blissful feeling of light, love and luck, and obtained frequent insights or information during prayers. Today I received the interesting insight that it can be beautiful if we all aim ourselves completely towards our higher aspects. But, that is not what its all about. I reached the illumination that the divine wished that we would have experiences in which we learn about life in all its qualities, that we learn what the impact of our choices can be, in short that we reach our potential of growth as a splendid flower. We do not need to be shrinking violets, in a corner, wanting to be good and beautiful out of love

for God but if we are a large, gnarled oak, with many branches and leaves, we also come close to God's wishes. The divine, the contact by means of prayer and faith, is a resource and a source of strength, and if we learn about the Love for God, this development can lead to God's growing satisfaction concerning how we try to reach this aim: to stand before His face and reach out for His hand as our greatest friend and our highest Self. Now I am only concerned with our people on this earth. How it is in other worlds I cannot say. Perhaps I learnt that from the Theosophy, the Sufism, Freemasonry, in the School of Vsevolod, and on my own path, and that is present in my consciousness.

I am very happy with this insight. I will work further and I feel God is now near, as my Master. What does this mean? Ultimate, complete freedom? That term is something I need to examine still more closely, but it feels like this. It is freedom and responsibility for one's own choices and their impact. Freedom even to not do well, freedom to live according to the standards of others, freedom of a strictly personal contact with God, as the Beloved, the Friend and the Master. Is this the awareness of the Cosmic People that we are?

Yesterday evening there was something special in the atmosphere, something of light and love. I wondered if it had something to do with the visit of Pope Benedict XVI to Southern Germany. I felt a very special link with him from the moment that he came into the picture. This contact arose when I accidentally saw him for the first time on Italian television (RAI) during the burial of the previous pope. He gave communion to the faithful on the square, I did not yet know who he was and I watched. Then I saw that he emanated light on administering communion, by means of his hands. I was touched by this and said to Georgy: `This will be the next pope!' It was Cardinal Ratzinger, who indeed some time later became Pope Benedict XVI. Up to a number of weeks afterwards I had been inspired and thought that he perhaps would revive Christianity in the

Western world by this means. Fortunately I understand Italian, so that I could follow speeches on Italian television easily. Is he able to give me the direction to the divine world of Christianity? I know that I must take the `leap' into the inner condition, from the suffocating personal, material world, to the light world that is incredibly fuller and more massive. I have recently had a lot of difficulty with Vsevolod. I still do not understand where he wants to lead the people of the School. That he gives them energy for working on their personal karma is a very good thing and also that he advises everyone to become a member of the Orthodox Church. They can get `spiritual protection' there. I don't really know, however, whether I can trust him. The fact is, however, that all my life I have had a certain aversion to so-called teachers, whoever they may be. I knew that I could learn something from them, on a temporary basis, but did not under any circumstances wish to be led astray from my inner self, my own consciousness and intuition, in short my inner freedom. My inner self has always been my feedback point, and I realised that with gratitude.

* * *

Chapter 10. Faust in the twenty first century. The new Hermeticism: the magician seeking God

In order to get a clear picture of the School of Vsevolod, I dived into books concerning the history and consistency of Hermeticism, Christianity, the Renaissance, Faust and eventually: the School. After reading The Elixir and the Stone, concerning the world of magic, the occult and unknown powers, written by Michael Baigent and Richard Leigh, my enthusiasm concerning the greater insight I received became even stronger. It became clear to me that the Faust figure already existed before time, that Alexandria was the cradle and Hermes, three times Great, the inspirer, and that his image was always changing, from the magician of natural powers and tricks, via the Renaissance magician, via Goethe's Faust, the magician who did not go under, but was given a new chance, to the image proposed by of the writers of the modern times in our history, of that is the magician who is in search of God. Formerly there was no question of this, partly due to the hostile attitude of the Catholic church, which assumed that it was the only institution that was allowed to spread knowledge and wisdom. When book-printing was invented a revolutionary change came to this situation: everyone could now read what he or she wanted.

After an age-long battle of science with philosophy, the official religion and arts for the sovereignty over Western civilisation and society, the scientist was, after the 2nd World War, the 'new' magician. In the sixties of the 20th century there was a new development, a revival of the occult, the underlying strength aimed at values, orienting oneself again towards integration, completeness, organism and synthesis. It was also called: Jung and that 'mystic rubbish'. this was looked at sceptically because of the self-centred aspect. Esotericism or New Age affectation became a source of derision. It concerned however a type of revolution, the type that the Renaissance had characterised, a revolution in attitude and values, in consciousness itself, in views and in the interaction with reality. Much was due to a corpus within 'esoteric' learning, which is indicated with the term 'hermeticism'. This emphasises among other things the mutual solidarity between several types of wisdom.

In that sense the revolution in the sixties that took place can consciously, however, be seen hermetically. The development of science had however been fragmented after 1945. Too large specialisations, no cross-connections. Whoever looked to Goethe, Balzac, Tolstoi, Dostojevski, Proust etc. for advice, found a more complete perspective and explicit references to hermeticism. In Lawrence Durrell one came up against references, for the first time, to the Corpus Hermeticum and the names of Paracelsus and Agrippa. In his Alexandria Quartet he gave a romanticised description of Alexandria and we became acquainted for the first time with the cradle of hermeticism. And therefore also with the most 'hermetic' of all spiritual disciplines, that of alchemy, as a complex and symbolic system that uses sexuality as a metaphor for art, art as a metaphor for sexuality and both as metaphors for a form of self-transformation. Then Jung came into the picture. The exciting discovery of hermeticism was that from this perspective one could see knowledge and reality, just like one could see the earth from space, in other words as seamless, entirely integrated. From this perspective we found the binding links between diverse disciplines and study areas, which were artificially separated, fragmented and isolated by the university itself. But at the same time hermeticism anticipated more than one abstraction, it offered empirical insights into the way magic is used, almost always a malicious form of magic, and became exploited within modern Western society, for corrupt aims. It became, at least in the modern world, a metaphor for certain misleading types of manipulation, for the art of 'letting things happen' in a manner which was hostile to the hermeticists themselves.

The Renaissance was rooted in values that were later called 'humanistic'. Yet the true impulse thus proved, eventually, to be really 'magic'. Now the 'universal genius', had still to be found, the character that would embody posterity. We found him between the 'magicians of the Renaissance', in a fictitious form, within a strictly Christian moral context, in the disguise of Marlowe's Doctor Faustus. We found him in a more tolerant and more pleasant context in Goethe's Faustus. He represented the restlessness, curiosity, courage, hunger for knowledge, contempt for convention, everything that characterised our generation. Both Faustus's confront Western civilisation with an embodiment of his collective identity.
In contrast to Jesus Christ this figure does not try to lead others to God, nor does he try to reach unity with God himself. On the contrary, he wants nothing less than to become God himself. To achieve this he uses the technical resources of his time to call up an immense and still unused power, a power that, according to traditional, Christian morality, was 'infernal', 'demonic', 'diabolical' and 'satanic'. With this character Faustus made a pact. He will have access to

all sources and opportunities to examine and to map the unknown. In exchange for the fact that, at the end of the time allocated to him, he will gamble his soul. An important difference between Marlowe's sixteenth century version of the tale and that of Goethe, which was written at the end of the eighteenth and the beginning of the nineteenth century, is that at the end of Marlowe's play Faustus has sold his soul and that is permanent, irreversible. At the end of Goethe's poem, the selling of his soul, thanks to the mediation of 'das Ewigweibliche', is postponed as a result of which rescue and salvation are possible for Faustus. Now, in the twenty-first century, our civilisation has the possibility to write its own Faustus version. The question remains whether we do that in the manner of Marlowe or that of Goethe, or something completely new, the search for God.

And then I became absorbed in the book, entitled 'Saint Silouan, the Athonite', written by Archimandrite Sophrony. He wrote the following and this moved me deeply, because I have already experienced that the borders of my 'faith' are too restrictive, and that I must let that go and love God, that is all.

The comment of the Archimandrite concerns the following: 'Many philosophical theologians, who are really rationalists, achieve a super-rationality, we would say even a super-logical intellectual environment, but this super-logical environment is not yet the Divine world, but has been decided within the limits of human, created nature; and is as such accessible in its nature, it is accessible to intelligence in a natural way. Their rational perceptions are not appropriate within the framework of formal logic and they convert to the environment of meta-logics. Nevertheless, their perceptions really remain the result of intellectual activity.

The victory over restricted formal logic is the proof of a high intellectual culture, but it is not yet the 'true faith' and witness of the true presence of God. They witness only the beauty of what is created in the likeness of God, and because they enter this environment of the `silence of the spirit' for the first time, they experience a certain `mystic excitement'. They consider their perceptions as the experience of the mystic relationship with God, whereas they remain in reality still within the limits of created human nature. The reasoning spirit exceeds the limits of time and space and gives to the contemplator the feeling of eternal wisdom. These are the extreme limits that can send the reasoning spirit on journeys of its own, reaching natural development and introspection. This experience is in itself an experience of pantheistic order.

If man `has set limits around the waters, until light and darkness shall reach their limit.' (Job 26:10), then he witnesses the beauty of his own spirit, which many have seen as Godly. Light that is witnessed by them is light, but not true light, in which there is absolutely no darkness. It is, however, natural light of the spirit of created people to the image of God.

This light of the spirit, which in its value goes beyond all empirical knowledge, can rightly be called darkness, because it the darkness of abstraction or of the misery in which God is absent; and in this case, perhaps still more than in every other case, one must remind oneself of the words of the Lord: `take care, lest the light that is within you become darkness. ' (Luke 11:35). The first cosmic, prehistoric calamity, i.e. the fall of the morning star, of Lucifer, who became the darkness itself, was the consequence of the self-focused, egotistic infatuation with one's own beauty; a consideration that ends with self-deification.

One can then say: `But this is nevertheless terrible... Where, then, is the guarantee of a true relationship with God, to be distinguished from the dreamy, philosophical, pantheistic relationship? The saint Elder Silouan claims categorically, that love for one's enemies is such a guarantee, at a level that is subordinate to our logical control. He said: `The Lord is humble and mild and He loves His creation and there where the Spirit of the Lord is, there will irrevocably be a humble love for one's enemies and a prayer for the world. And if you do not have this love, then you must pray for this reason; and the Lord, Who has said: 'Pray, and you will receive, seek and you shall find' (Matth. 7:7), will grant it to you.

And nobody should venture to underestimate this 'psychological' law, because such a psychic state is the consequence of true Divine activity. God the Saviour saves the whole person, therefore not only the intelligence with the spirit. But also the psyche with the emotions, both the thinking being and the physical body, everything has been sanctified by God.

I was extremely moved. It seems as if I was liberated, because I had experienced this state already! To me it means that, whatever I do I cannot in fact become closer to God through my behaviour and by this I mean of course Jesus Christ, the Mother of God and the saints. But I also do not need to, I feel it is enough that my love and surrender to God is from my being and that the rest comes automatically. What a relief and how simple it actually is. I start praying and feel myself suddenly liberated and free, finding myself in the sunny light of the cosmos, I feel I've lost a thousand kilos, I no longer need that heavy, ponderous knowledge, which only increases the feeling of sin and guilt and the feeling of helplessness, because we are no saints, but creatures striving from the depths of the earth towards the light. I chose the path, this path of discovery, knowledge, human hierarchy, especially in spiritual and related organisations, striving to achieve something, yes, to be someone and always having the feeling of having failed. I let that go now, shaking off the illusions like old clothes and fly free like an eagle, high in air, to the sun and love... I am what I am, God loves me and I want to love Him also. This deserves a poem.

The eventual consequence is: complete surrender, Dear Lord, Thy will be done...

And then the prayer to my guardian angel follows: `Intercede for me to the Lord that he confirms me as his esteemed servant who is worthy of His goodness.

This is the task of humanity. When will we be worthy of His goodness? This goodness is there always... This means we have to work on ourselves, ennobling ourselves, seeking the guidelines for our lives in the Good, the Goodness of God, the Heart. This offers splendid panoramas for us, people: the growth towards inner and outward nobility, from the Spirit.

* * *

Chapter 11. Russian Orthodoxy - Thoughts

Yesterday, Sunday, I have for the first time in almost two years been in the orthodox church, with Father Nicholas. Although I have sung there since 1997 for seven years in the church choir and have learned many things about Russian religious matters, Georgy and I moved in January 2005 to the orthodox convent, where the liturgy is in Dutch. We are very pleased with this, especially as I had had enough of it, that everything was in Russian and I gradually felt more and more of an outsider. Furthermore, at the end of 2004 there was a slight conflict between us and Father Nicholas. Georgy went now and then to the church to go to confession and receive communion. We were very moved when a couple of months ago he said to Georgy that he wanted to ask for our forgiveness if he had acted in an incorrect manner towards us. Finally, yesterday there was a splendid service in the church, full of light and elevation of the soul, and we decided to stay till the end. The service here lasts longer than in the convent, because Father Nicholas follows the Russian monastic rules. Therefore we could kiss the cross in his hand at the farewell and then Father Nicholas looked affectionately at me and asked how I was, which I cannot forget. In fact I knew him, personally, only as a slightly barbaric Russian macho and I no longer needed that. But yesterday my heart melted and I felt connected with his church again. The seven years in which I have been involved there were also splendid and I have deeply penetrated into the Russian religious heart. I have a deep respect for the mystical in orthodoxy and it seems to me that this is one of the most important paths to God. Not in the sense of spiritual schools, which in my opinion begin with the viewpoint of earthly consciousness and this is possibly due to the consciousness of their students, but in the sense of the vision which I had in February 1997 during the service in an orthodox church, when we followed the icon painting course with icon painter Bernard Frinking there: it was as if in a flash a curtain was pulled aside and I saw large, splendid, light beings, were they angels? They had been involved in the church service and seemed in parallel to carry out the same liturgy.

Those ten days, during which we lived in the church and studied, have proven to be among the most important experiences in my life. Georgy had consequently developed into a respectable icon painter and a number of his icons hang in the church, dedicated to it, and I have given lectures concerning my inner and external experiences in `painting my first icon', among other things, at the Freemasons. At Plotinus Lodge I was then admitted to the master degree. A year ago I held the same lecture here at home for a group of people from the School, but this ended less well for me: I was extremely ill afterwards for two days. Supposedly this was the consequence of the psychic defence of a number of people and these `underground' attacks can be very nasty. Since then I have given no more lectures for people from the School. Unfortunately I must say that I do not have much affinity with people from the School, I am even a little frightened of them. Sometimes in their presence I feel a kind of knot in my stomach, though they are probably not aware of it.

In a Theosophy book I read something this morning that I found clarified a lot, simply with regard to my practical insight. It is a book by C. Jinarajadasa and is called `How we remember our past Lives'. it is the original edition of 1915 and has been printed in Adyar, Madras, India, the original headquarters of the `Theosophical Society', where I had been in 2000. It is not the aspect of reincarnation that captivated me, but the explanation concerning the soul and individuality, concerning the question of who am 'I'? Moreover, Georgy and I had recently translated the Dutch version of a Russian orthodox book concerning the existence of the soul, and this consistency seemed very interesting to me.

He writes that the 'I' of the average man or woman is hardly more than a collection of properties of sex, religion and nationality. But the soul is immortal, has no notion of time, as a result of which it ends up on the wrong track of youth and ageing. It is neither man nor woman, but develops in the best properties of both sexes. It is not Hindu, Buddhist, Christian or Moslem, because it lives in one divine life and that incorporates life according to its temperament. It is not Indian, English or American, because it belongs to absolutely no country whatsoever, although its outer sheath, the physical body, belongs to a certain race. It does not belong to a certain caste or class, because it knows that all are part of the One Life, and that for God no Brahman or Soedra, Jew or non-Jew, aristocrat or plebeian, exists.

During a certain period of time, the Soul sets a part of itself, the Personality, apart 'purely as an object for experience and experiment'. It observes life by means of its persona, the 'mask' of a child, youth or little girl, man or woman, bachelor, spinster or house keeper, old man or old woman. In the past its personalities were those of Lemurians or Atlantians, Hindus or Romans or Greeks, and it selects the best personalities and dismisses the rest. Literature, science, art, religion and civilisations are its school and its playground, workshop and study. Its nationalism concerns the indivisible Humanity and its religion is the cooperation with 'God's plan, which is evolution'. And it is this Soul that has had lives. Whoever asks 'why do I not remember my previous lives?' must do this by means of his personality. The body of that personality has a brain, but the memories of previous lives have not been stored in it. Those memories are found in the Divine Being, who does not belong to a certain time, religion or country. To remember the previous lives of the Soul, the brain must act as a mirror in which the memories of the Soul are reflected. But before this is the case, the various preconceptions over mortality, time, sex, religion, colour or caste, are removed. As long as we have not done that we maintain barriers between our higher selves and our lower selves.

Well, that brings our consciousness to a certain level of clarity, and we obtain an instrument to increasingly purify our relationship with God.

I will use it gratefully. Thank you, Theosophy! I say this for all the years that I was involved with you, and I still have the honour of calling myself a Theosophist.

For some years now I have prayed every morning and evening from the prayer book of the orthodox Tradition. That has become my habit and I notice that saying these prayers consciously removes all kinds of barriers from my consciousness and allows me to see the things clearly. It says: `... in secret Ye maketh my wisdom known... (Ps.50: 8)

By saying the Lord's Prayer continuously, if I cannot sleep, I receive a connection of light, and then it is as if this prayer is a flowing river of light, which flows steadily further, even if I do not pray. Therefore this praying continues. You then feel quiet and certain and life is no longer so distressing. I notice that this fear comes from the persona, as Jinarajadasa describes it, and if I continue to pray the Lord's Prayer, I feel something marvellous: my `I' is surrounded by a light, golden energy and that energy is eternal. This energy helps me to illuminate the energy that I call `I', because that same 'I' appears as a dark cluster, probably of energy. That illumination that eases and subsequently solves my problems and fears and then I realise that I am worrying for nothing. That is all just a question of illusions and anxious thinking. But we cannot escape from it, because we are that `I'! That is what we think in any case, and that is therefore the great illusion.

I understand still better how those mechanisms work and have developed methods of coping with this and not burdening myself with trivial problems. You learn that you have a right to sit quietly in your own place, being in hara, focused on the golden inner self, and find the source of your life there. Therefore the instrument, the `I' must erase his own importance and follow Saint Silouan as much as possible, who says: `Keep your spirit in hell, and do not despair'. He meant this as consolation, because God is there always.

Today something marvellous happened during morning prayer. I feel all of a sudden transported to ancient Egypt, I receive an initiation and fly inwardly towards the freedom of the cosmos and the light. The sun is shining and there is desert around me, but also a white building. I am in a state of bliss. I am, I think, in a temple of Isis and Osiris, because those names come to me. I see aristocratic grandeur in me and in the invisible figures around me. But still more typical is that I see that undergoing the initiation and my

Christian morning prayer are no different. There is the same light, the same depth, there is also the notion of Christ, in short: there is no inner difference in experience and depth between my orthodox morning prayer in the year of Our Lord 2006, and a situation of initiation, perhaps 2006 before Christ. This I have never experienced in this way. It is a fantastic experience. I hope to be able to hold on to it for a long time to come.

It is miraculous. By means of the Orthodox church I have been able to penetrate deeply into the Christian faith. I already had a certain affinity with it and this has acquired depth in the last eight to ten years. It occurs to me that in my inner self a dimension has appeared that during prayer I have been able to experience the Divine and the saints almost in three dimensions. The Mother of God has come closer to me, and a couple of days ago an idea came to me, with the question regarding whether I wanted to belong to her following. I naturally answered 'yes', although I have no idea what it means. It is all present in my heart. But now most miraculously of all: my experience, during prayer, concerning my initiation in Egypt, gives me an overwhelmingly liberating, spiritual and perhaps also material view of the Living Universe. I realise that my mystic experiences in orthodox Christianity are perhaps universal. Because this depth was also present in the experience in Egypt, and if I further reflect on this I realise that I also worship Christ in the form of Osiris, Brahma, Allah, Avilokateshvara... and many others whose names I cannot think of presently. I also worship the Mother of God in Isis (if I am wrong, this will, however, become clear to me) and, possibly in the other existing religions, Divine Mother. The Mother of God is for me a very special being: it seems to me that she fulfils a major role as an aid to purifying our personality, as I have already described. She is Commiseration and Divine Maternal Love and is constantly sought to this end by the faithful. She is thus closer to them and communes with millions. It seems that she is continuously called upon for aid and as a result is also very close to us. I feel a deep connection with her in recent times and I recently had an experience, in which I was an ecstatic, light being, who carried out tasks in this earthly life while filled with joy. I do not know if they were tasks from the Mother of God, but it concerns that splendid experience of the highest form of happiness, light, creativity and energy, whereby my heart was full of love.

By means of this insight I feel myself at one with the depth of all major religions and I am very grateful to Christianity, as by means of my knowledge of it I have been able to experience this depth and the universality of these deep images and experiences. Now I think I know the reason why I left the Sufi Circle, the unity of the religions was made too formal there and, insofar as I know, there was nobody who had investigated even one of these religions in depth. That was also always my objection against the way the Universal Worship was carried out: slightly superficial. If I am right, those who also profess to membership of the other religions experience this depth, if they at least delve into the depth, into the mystical aspects of it. It seems as if I experience an extension of my consciousness in this depth and that makes me extraordinarily happy. It feels as if I am 'normal' at last.

I realise, that if I say my orthodox prayers, I pray also to the universal of these images in the other major religions and that they are indeed there! Is that not splendid, is that not fantastic!

Hopefully this insight and this experience gives me the strength and the opportunities in our world to work, either practically and/or spiritually, to 'incarnate' this Truth in the material existence of the everyday, in people and in their activities. This is possible if I practise creativity, self discipline, charity and respect and try to reach others to help the consciousness of the heart and to let them know what their task is in this earthly life: to find this Light and to realise our divine task. The task to do God's will on earth and to fully commit ourselves to God and to become what we are meant to be.

Humility

Since last Sunday, the service in the church, I feel a golden light, as a tender wave, it is liberating and delivering and makes me humble. That humility moves me deeply, more so I think because now at last I dare to be humble. In `horizontal' life this sometimes means that others profit from you or manipulate you. But now the situation is different, I dare to stand in this gentle light with that golden wave, and I feel that I should give myself more and more. This loving, delicate, golden wave should take the reins of my life in hand. Because of this my intuition will lead me and not my fears. It demands some audacity for me to deliver myself entirely to this. But I would not want it to be any other way. I feel gentle and sweet, I deliver myself and that brings a deep feeling of happiness. I have not been fully subjected to it, because I can focus at any moment on the hard, `horizontal' world. I must train myself to coordinate myself on this more often. Is it my soul? Is this the Mother of God aura? I feel linked to Her recently as if She appears in the three-dimensional world. During prayers I feel this depth more often as if I am in the presence of real persons, the Mother of God or the saints. That makes praying much easier, because you seem to have a real connection at that moment.

Prayer

Today I read 'Elder Silouan, the Athonite' concerning prayer. It concerns the aim, in other words the hesychastic prayer, giving oneself over to Christ by means of the prayer: `Lord Jesus Christ, Son of God, have mercy on me, a sinner'. The illusion offers many traps such as the rationalism that applies to a lot of types of meditation, prayers to divine images which one creates oneself, instead of realising that God has created us, the ultimate trap being when one considers oneself to be God. He points the way to the darkness of abstraction or of the destitution in which God is not present and the words of the Lord: ` Therefore, take care, lest the light that is within you become darkness.' (Luke 11:35). The first cosmic prehistoric calamity, i.e. the fall of the morning star, of Lucifer, who became darkness, was the consequence of the self-focused love of one's own beauty; a consideration which ended in self deification.

And then the splendid answer to the question: `Where is the guarantee of true communion with God then, for the understanding of the imaginary, philosophical, pantheistic communion? Saint Elder Silouan claimed that love for the enemy is such a guarantee, at a level that is subordinate to our logical control. He said: `The Lord is humble and kind and He loves His creation and there where the spirit of the Lord is, there will irrevocably be a humble love for the enemies and a prayer for the world. And if you do not have this love, then you must pray for this reason; and the Lord, Who has said: `Ask, and it shall be given to you. Seek, and you shall find. Knock, and it shall be opened to you.' (Matth.7: 7), will grant it to you. Such a spiritual state is the consequence of true Divine action.

I am learning from this book that the spiritual state causes uncountable misunderstandings in images and ideas, to which one attributes a quality that is not there. What is the usefulness of this? Humility, and if I succeed in this I will be relieved of a heavy inner burden. I continue to try, with much gratitude that I am a healthy and vigorous lass of forty-five...

Yesterday there was a splendid liturgy in the convent. The Belgian priest, Father Thimo has replaced Father Born on his departure. It seems as if he brings the lifting, golden sky down, to us, during the service. Tears came to my eyes. He is a powerful individual and abbot of a Belgian monastery and archimandrite. He hears confession in a very non-conventional manner and says that God will forgive, but that we must first find the roots, the cause of that to which we confess. You leave him giggling a little, but you know what you have to do. I had expressed my contrition concerning the fact that I frequently feel irritated by people and that I reject that attitude in myself. He said: `God forgives you naturally', but instructed me to become humbler. Completely true and I will pay attention to it. Why do I have little patience with people? While I gladly want to have contact with others. Perhaps I have too little energy to carry out my good intentions, but I do not like nonsense and crudeness, at least what I see as such. Then my interest disappears and I go my own way, a little angry. Well, we are going to do something about that.

After the service we went together, with Marina and others to drink coffee. I told her at a given moment, when she spoke about her enneagram course, that this working on herself with the aim of overcoming the lower individuality and reaching the Divine, in my opinion, is the terrain of the Mother of God. I told her that I have learned this from praying that the prayer contains a lot of information and if you are open in the correct manner during praying, you can learn just about everything and it is possible to understand everything concerning your own situation and its relationship to a higher consciousness. By higher I mean God, Jesus Christ, the Mother of God and the saints. This knowledge concerns Light and the degree of Light, concerns Love and the degree of Love, concerns communication with the Divine, and all this gives an emotional picture of yourself with respect to this Light and this Love and how you can be guided through this.

Also concerning the knowledge supplied to you by the Divine, this can even be read in Psalm 51:8: `For behold, you have loved truth. The obscure and hidden things of your wisdom, you have manifested to me.'. And further: `In my hearing, you will grant gladness and rejoicing. And the bones that have been humbled will exult.'. (Ps 51:10) Is there an inspiration greater than experiencing this joy and exhilaration, as I have tried to describe here, and letting go of your own small priorities for the sake of this love? Your own purification remains of course a difficult matter, but you obtain insight...

Light - the winter Saint John celebrations at the Freemasons

'And the light shines in the darkness, and the darkness did not comprehend it.' (John 1:5)
Darkness has its own scheme. It is apparently not pleased with that light... What is light to me? Light in itself means less to me than its association with warmth, the warm fire that gives light, for example ... Are light and heat (fire) connected to each other? Light that is associated with fire gives me security, intimacy, love, faith, togetherness, unity, luck. Sometimes I need light in order to shine it on something. Then the subject must become clear or transparent, but then I feel no warmth.
I can do a lot with that clarity and knowledge which I obtain by this means (that can be a little cool), I can make connections, draw parallels and discover all kinds of new things, I can convince other people who do not have so much light etc., in short: light provides possibilities. I see it better, but I feel no warmth, no happiness, no oneness with all that is.

Why do I want warmth? Will Light have an inside and an outside? An internal and an external? A warm and cold side? There was something in me, perhaps deep in my soul, that would know that happiness exists and that belongs entirely to me, a type of birth right, and something desperate in me wanted to retrieve that happiness? Do I want warmth for this reason? Can my darkness understand the Light nevertheless? Do I recognise something?

Light from the sun warms me, and ensures that I see more clearly ... I could see nothing until that light was there, then obscurity was all around and everything was vague and cold. But then the sun came up and there was warmth in me and outside me. I seized that sunlight and something in me came back to life. I have a strong relationship with the sun...

If I feel love, faith, togetherness this way, then I feel that in my heart. Then there is fire in my heart, and would that cause light? Or the other way around? The sun makes my heart warm and provides light for me to see.

You understand now, however, what light at Winter St. Jan is for me: lighting the fire: warmth in Thine heart and mine...

Control over thoughts

Isn't it nevertheless difficult to keep your thoughts under control. I realise, that our entire life is bombarded by ideas from the spiritual atmosphere around us or within ourselves, it is like grey mops swirling around with hardly any meaning for the present. In fact, no meaning at all. Christian ascetics teach us to repel such images, that conjure up such thoughts so that it has no impact and it is gone! That is not possible for me, but the fact that I realise is already a lot. I frequently think that `I seem mad' if I sit and spin around in such a mop and let my energy ebb away. Without those thoughts my life is fantastic. I thank God for that regularly. Now to my own realisation ...

Concerning pride

This morning, during prayer, it struck me just how proud I am! Suddenly I realised that even my attempts at spirituality and `limitless knowledge' means nothing, that people are `nothing' and are in God's hands. Being at the mercy disturbs man, he wants to be someone, to be God. He wants be the divine spark in itself. Was this the misfortune of Lucifer? He wants to be equal to God, and people, in his search to which He is, go astray thereby also always. The way I now feel, sad, totally `demotivated' because of my own useless attempts to reach God, feeling worthless and like I must hand myself over simply to God. I realise that Christianity is based on this. How does this work then with the hermeticist? How does it work with the Christian hermeticist? The hermeticist that wants to follow Christ? Is hermeticism the way of Faust? Yes, thus, when one continues to cling to the knowledge of material, all material aspects.

Is there a moment when the hermeticist jumps over the abyss? Has to jump? Should hermeticism be considered as a science, the same as all sciences? When a hermeticist dares to 'leap' into the illuminating, spiritual world, he will see all his achievements in accumulating knowledge as being useless, because on the other side he will receive spiritual knowledge, and then I think of my vision during the Russian orthodox liturgy in 1997.

Also alchemy can be seen as a normal science, even when it coincides with seeking inner gold, to one's deepest self. Because then one is still on the material side, but then very refined.

In my vision I saw that the spiritual world provides cosmic knowledge that is similar to hermeticism, but at the same time totally different from it, because our perception has received another quality by means of our transformation and then we will encounter true spiritual laws.

About life after death

During prayer I received an insight: I saw the energy field, which we actually are. I saw our bodies, which are perishable. The prayers of Christianity lead us to focus on the worlds of energy, and for this reason the spiritual world obviously exists. After our death we become our energy body and if we have aimed ourselves towards God during our life, we become directly more 'consciously' in contact with the spiritual world. Our material body thinks that it is crazy to pray to something that is invisible to the physical eye and praying in the Western world for a large part has been lost. During prayer, if this happens in the correct manner, therefore if our heart takes part in a conversation, we make the connection with the saints to whom we pray. Where the energy world exists, the spiritual world therefore also exists. The most beautiful thing that I might achieve is to consciously continue to aim at that inner depth, all day long, that develops in me. In that inner depth I feel that I have contact with the higher worlds, and those I call God, Jesus Christ, the Mother of God and the saints. For this reason I receive so much insight during prayer, perhaps I am in conversation with God or the saint. This has to do directly with the afterlife. I only assume this myself, and I am not even speaking of the spirits of the deceased, because I am aware that this is specific knowledge. Theosophy has taught me a lot concerning the various stages of the afterlife.

But I now want to only concentrate on my own relation to the energy worlds, the rest will follow, the deducing and combining, the deeper development of insights.

The spiritual world, the existence of it, is therefore a fact. The point is to find the correct path in this, to follow the correct route to God, Whom I seek. Because there are also enough pitfalls. It is important and a privilege to seek that route if we are ourselves in our material body, therefore if we are incarnated. Why? Because for us being incarnated in physical bodies is an anchor and gives us strength and stability to find this route, in our own manner, and in an effective manner to follow it.

* * *

CHAPTER 12. CONCLUSION. MONDAY, 5 MARCH 2007

Yesterday was the last meeting of this year with the Russians and the School. Georgy and I were able to introduce the showpiece of our published books, this being the album with full-colour symbolic, alchemical images, which had been devised by Kliment.
Vsevolod seemed very happy with this book, as were the students of the School. A couple of errors have been found, which we will proceed to correct, and, very charmingly our Swedish Anna appeared enthusiastic about these slips-up, because they are now `collectors items', because errors in well-known books make such a copy much more valuable… Even my son Edwin expressed himself positively concerning it and asked for it as a gift for his birthday. I told Vsevolod this, and also that Edwin has read the other books. Vsevolod considered this as proof, that if even Edwin appreciated it (!), the outside world is therefore interested in our books. In these last couple of meetings with Vsevolod and Kliment I feel good, relaxed and open. I feel myself more incorporated in the weave of the School. That is very beautiful and Vsevolod and Kliment created that. This situation has no more connection with the pain that I had felt for a number of years due to them. The exhilaration of Vsevolod yesterday for our book touched me and I had a warm feeling towards him and Kliment. I feel more than ever that Georgy and I have a task, and that is: publishing books. We have grounded the message of the School with that, now and for future times. Georgy and I attended few meetings in the last few years, we were much too busy with Georgy's professional life in the Netherlands and publishing the books by Kliment through Georgy's publishing house and of the Orthodox Christian books throuhg my publishing house. Putting into practice our spiritual knowledge is both exciting and creative, right up to the present day! We feel very inspired by the mysticism of Russian orthodoxy and thereby establish also our links to these sources.

My background in Theosophy, Sufism, and Freemasonry, for example, ensured that I have come to feel strong in myself, I remain critical and yet benevolent and adjust my pace when I see that this is necessary. Vsevolod indicated that their School belongs to the stellar tradition and its universality attracts me. It is also not clear to me whether this universal orientation is still in practice now in the original manner, as sometimes certain groups of students give me the impression that they are busy consuming in 'beautiful fenced-in, safe gardens'. And they can sometimes act with a very mysterious air....

I am grateful for all the knowledge, which I have been able to accumulate and feel that the contents of my rucksack of spiritual knowledge was also further completed by the School, which is of great value for me. I think that, personally seen, my greatest problem is still my Cinderella identification, the inheritance of the Japanese camp. But now, in my seventies, I have over the course of the years acquired a lot more self-knowledge, so this problem does not arise anymore and I continue to move in the direction of my already favourite areas. Georgy and I have always held the ideal that we want to do `something useful for humanity' and we more or less do that. According to an astrologer I have done much in my previous incarnations for humanity, but in this incarnation my task is no longer to work for the message of others, but to allow this to come from myself now. Perhaps I have succeeded.

* * *

www.ingramcontent.com/pod-product-compliance
Lightning Source LLC
LaVergne TN
LVHW041842070526
838199LV00045BA/1396